60 Catholics Who Changed the World

by

Gerard M. Verschuuren

En Route Books and Media, LLC
St. Louis, MO

En Route Books and Media, LLC
5705 Rhodes Avenue
St. Louis, MO 63109

Cover credit: TJ Burdick

LCCN: 2020936482
ISBN-13: 978-1-95-246405-8

Copyright © 2020 Gerard M. Verschuuren
All rights reserved.

Table of Contents

PREFACE i
1. ALBERT THE GREAT: SCIENCE & RELIGION 1
2. ALCUIN OF YORK: SCHOOLS 4
3. ANGELICA, MARY: MASS COMMUNICATION 7
4. ANSELM OF CANTERBURY: SLAVERY 13
5. ATHANASIUS OF ALEXANDRIA: ONE GOD 16
6. BARAT, MADELEINE-SOPHIE: EDUCATION OF WOMEN 22
7. BEDE THE VENERABLE: HISTORY 25
8. BELLARMINE, ROBERT: HUMAN RIGHTS 28
9. BENEDICT OF NURSIA: HOSPITALS 33
10. BOSCO, GIOVANNI: URBANIZATION 38
11. BRANDSMA, TITUS: FREEDOM OF PRESS 41
12. CAFASSO, JOSEPH: PRISONS 47
13. CAMILLUS DE LELLIS: RED CROSS 50
14. CANISIUS, PETER: THE CATECHISM 53
15. CARREL, ALEXIS: MIRACLES 59
16. CATHERINE OF SIENA: FEMINISM 65
17. CHESTERTON, G. K.: COMMON SENSE 68
18. CLAVER, PETER: SLAVE TRADE 71
19. CONSTANTINE THE GREAT: A BREAKTHROUGH 74
20. COPERNICUS, NICOLAUS: HELIOCENTRISM 77
21. CYRIL AND METHODIUS: THE VERNACULAR 80

22. DAMIEN DE VEUSTER: LEPROSY 83
23. DAY, DOROTHY: SOCIAL JUSTICE 86
24. DOWLING, EDWARD: ADDICTIONS 89
25. DREXEL, KATHARINE: HUMAN DIVERSITY 92
26. DUHEM, PIERRE: SCIENCE ROOTS 95
27. FRANCIS OF ASSISI: MOTHER EARTH 101
28. FRANCIS XAVIER: MISSIONARIES 107
29. GONZALEZ, ROQUE: JESUIT REDUCTIONS 113
30. GREENE, GRAHAM: NOVELS 116
31. GREGORY THE GREAT: PAPAL AUTHORITY 121
32. GREGORY VII: CHURCH AND STATE 126
33. GREGORY XIII: GREGORIAN CALENDAR 132
34. GUTENBERG, JOHANNES: PRINTING PRESS 138
35. HIERONYMUS, EUSEBIUS: THE BIBLE 141
36. HILDEGARD OF BINGEN: USING TALENTS 147
37. IGNATIUS OF ANTIOCH: CATHOLIC OR
    CHRISTIAN? 153
38. IGNATIUS OF LOYOLA: GOD'S SOLDIERS 156
39. ISIDORE OF SEVILLE: SCHOOLING 162
40. JOHN PAUL II: COMMUNISM 165
41. JUSTIN THE MARTYR: FAITH AND REASON 171
42. LANDSTEINER, KARL: BLOOD TRANSFUSIONS 177
43. LEMAÎTRE, GEORGES: BIG BANG 180
44. LEO XIII: SOCIAL TEACHING 186
45. LEWIS, C.S.: APOLOGETICS 192
46. MARITAIN, JACQUES: HUMAN RIGHTS 198
47. MCCORVEY, NORMA: ABORTION 204
48. MCLUHAN, MARSHALL: SOCIAL MEDIA 207
49. MENDEL, GREGOR: GENETICS 213
50. MORE, THOMAS: RELIGIOUS LIBERTY 216
51. PASTEUR, LOUIS: MICRO-ORGANISMS 222
52. PAUL OF TARSUS: APOSTLE WITHOUT BORDERS . 225
53. PAUL VI: SEXUAL REVOLUTION 231
54. PIUS XII: NOT HITLER'S POPE 237

55. RYAN, JOHN AUGUSTAN: MINIMUM WAGE 243
56. SCHUMACHER, E.F.: SMALL IS BEAUTIFUL 246
57. SEMMELWEIS, IGNAZ: WASHING HANDS 249
58. SERRA, JUNÍPERO: ONE HUMAN RACE 255
59. TERESA OF CALCUTTA: WHO ARE THE POOREST? 258
60. THOMAS AQUINAS: NO DOUBLE TRUTH 264

CONCLUSION 270
INDEX 271
PRAISE FOR THE BOOK 276
ABOUT THE AUTHOR 276

Preface

This book is about sixty Catholics who changed the world we live in now. Probably every religion or nation can come up with members who have "changed" the world in some way. Obviously, we mean that they have changed the world for the better. Unfortunately, many too have made the world worse.

Why only mention Catholics in this book, you may ask. Well, first of all, I am a Catholic myself, who is proud of what my fellow Catholics did for the world. Second, what they all have in common is that they were inspired by Jesus Christ to do what they actually did for the world—Jesus was their driving force with his Good News of the Gospel. Third, religion (or lack thereof) is an important part of what makes us who we are and makes us do what we do—including Catholicism. Fourth, the Catholic Church has a longstanding and outstanding tradition that makes for a powerful source of innovations for the world. Each one of these sixty Catholics made a significant contribution.

Did others make great changes to this world? Absolutely they did, but let someone else write that story. Are some Catholics missing in this series? Definitely! Some have changed the world more than others, so it is hard to decide who should be in and who might be left out. Besides, my selection of influential Catholics is personal and undoubtedly biased. Also, there are probably also many Catholics from our current era that you think should be mentioned in this book. But those still need to be tested for how their impact will hold out in the time ahead of us. Only history can tell, after the dust has settled, whether and how they actually changed the world.

The ones who did end up in this book had quite a bearing on how the world is now. They should not be forgotten and they deserve our gratefulness. This book will help you to find out why.

1

Albert the Great: Science & Religion

There is this old Western in which one cowboy says to the other: "This town ain't big enough for both of us. One of us has to leave." The Boston College philosopher Peter Kreeft uses this story to show how many people nowadays feel about the relationship between science and religion—one of them has to leave. If you agree with this, then you probably think also that religion must be the one to leave, for the more science advances, the more religion loses. In the view of these people, scientific expansion means religious withdrawal—so religion must be on its way out whenever science makes progress. They declare science as the winner, so religion has to leave town.

Obviously, this view sees science and religion as competitors that vie for the same prize, so when one of the two wins, the other loses. Can that be true? No, this idea was already exposed as flawed some nine centuries ago by Albert the Great (1193-1280).

Albert the Great, also known as *Albertus Magnus,* was probably born in Lauingen (now in Bavaria), since he called himself "Albert of Lauingen"—but this might simply be a family name. It is very likely that Albert was educated at the University of Padua, where he received instruction in Aristotle's writings.

In 1223, he joined the Dominican Order and studied theology at Bologna. Selected to fill the position of lecturer at Cologne, Germany, where the Dominicans had a house, he taught for several years there, as well as in Regensburg, Freiburg and Strasbourg.

Albert's writings were collected in 1899 and went to thirty-eight volumes. These displayed his prolific habits and encyclopedic knowledge of topics as diverse as logic, theology, botany, geography, astronomy, mineralogy, chemistry, zoology, physiology, justice and law. Apparently, he was what we call now a *polymath* or a *homo universalis*—a person whose expertise spans a significant number of different subject areas. He did not have that very narrow, specialized scope that most scientists are known for today. As a matter of fact, he was highly qualified to judge how religion and science are related to each other because he was no stranger to either one.

On the one hand, he was an excellent philosopher and theologian. As a philosopher, he was the first man to comment on virtually every existing work of Aristotle, opening up the Greek philosophers to scrutiny. Without his commentaries and his influence on his pupils, modern philosophy would be a very different monster today and one might even say that the Age of Enlightenment may never have happened, as it was, in part, a rebellion against the medieval philosophies of the likes of Albert.

On the other hand, he was also an exceptional scientist for his time. We have to realize, though, that the term "science" [*scientia*] simply meant "knowledge" at the time, and the term "scientist" did not even exist until William Whewell coined it in 1833. Yet, Albert was a scientist as we understand it today. Through logic and observation, he wrote in-depth works on such varied subjects mentioned above that were within his range of knowledge. Albert had actually quite a track record for his time: he discovered the element arsenic; he experimented with photosensitive chemicals, including silver nitrate; and he made disciplined observations in plant anatomy and animal embryology. In short, Albert's knowledge of the natural sciences was considerable and for the age remarkably accurate. His productiveness in every department was just great. He emphasized that experiment is the only safe guide in scientific investigations.

Albert saw no conflict between his scientific activities and his religious beliefs. He did not consider science and religion as competitors of each other. Put in terms of the old Western, why would one of them have to leave? Well, neither one has to leave; the "town" is big enough for both science and religion. They're not competing for a prize that only one can have. Instead, both science and religion should respect each other's territory and authority.

Why? Because there are so many questions science could never answer. Science knows nothing about God, can settle nothing about morals, and knows nothing of life's meaning. Limiting truth to scientifically verified facts automatically closes the door for any facts and truths about God, about morality, or about the meaning of life. For Albert, that's unacceptable, unreasonable, and even impossible. That's something we can learn from him.

Albert the Great is one of those Catholics who changed the world we live in. He cleared the path for a peaceful, and necessary, co-existence between science and religion.

2

Alcuin of York: Schools

We all want to learn. When we set the first steps in life, we are already embarking on a journey of exploration. The question "Why?" is on every child's tongue. From an early age on, we are masters of questioning and reasoning. Our capacity for reasoning sets us apart from the rest of the animal world. Pope John Paul II, in his Encyclical *Fides et Ratio* ("Faith and Reason"), went even as far as saying, "the human being is by nature a philosopher." Do we need to be trained for this? No we don't, it's partly "inborn." On the other hand, yes we do, for we can do much better if we are "schooled" to do better. Therefore, we need schools in the fight against illiteracy.

There may be many reasons why some people hate school, but that doesn't change the fact that we want to improve the educational system and want to establish it in countries that don't have one. We want to eradicate child labor in order for children to have a chance to benefit from education. Lack of education is one of the main causes of poverty and one of the main reasons why people can't find a job and make a decent living. But schools are not part of nature—they have to be implemented. The person who played an important role in all of this was Alcuin of York (735-804).

Alcuin of York was the rector of the cathedral school at York, in England, where he had studied himself. An innovative educator, he improved the school, made its library one of England's best, and attracted outstanding students. Therefore, he was invited by King Charlemagne to become a leading teacher at the Carolingian court in Aachen, Germany. As head of the palace school, Alcuin elevated the culture at court and sponsored educational enterprises throughout the entire Carolingian empire.

The size of the empire at its inception in 800 was around 1,112,000 square kilometers (429,000 sq miles), with a population of between 10 and 20 million people. To the south it bordered Spain; to the north it bordered the kingdom of the Danes; to the west it had a short land border with Brittany; and to the east it had a long border with the Slavs.

It was around the turn of the 8th century that Charlemagne presided over a revival of learning in his empire, from where it would spread to other parts of Europe, and eventually to other parts of the world. As a first step, Charlemagne decreed that each monastery and Cathedral chapter establish a school. Then, a plan for universal elementary education was projected. It was decreed in the year 802 that "everyone should send his son to study letters, and that the child should remain at school with all diligence until he should become well instructed in learning." Following the decrees of the Council of Vaison, a primary school was to be established in every town and village. In all of this, Alcuin played a key role.

It is not quite clear to what extent Alcuin deserves credit for the organization of the vast educational system which was thus set up, comprising a central higher institution, the Palace School, a number of subordinate schools of the liberal arts scattered throughout the country, and schools for the common people in every city and village. His hand is nowhere visible in the series of legislative enactments referred to, but scholars have no doubt that he had much to do with the instigation, if not with the framing, of these laws. It has rightly been stated that "The voice is the voice of Charles, but the hand is the hand of Alcuin."

Of his work as an educator and text book writer, it may be said that Alcuin had the largest share in the movement for the revival of learning which distinguished the age in which he lived, and which made possible the great intellectual renaissance of three centuries later, often referred to as the Carolingian Renaissance. It is for his vast efforts as an educational reformer that history recognizes Alcuin as "the schoolmaster of Europe," and eventually of the world.

Alcuin is another one of those Catholics who changed the world we live in. He made education a goal for every citizen, not just the elite. Blame him if you still hate school.

3

Angelica, Mary: Mass Communication

Probably not a day goes by that we don't watch or read what mass media channels such as television, newspapers and the internet want to tell us. They are our main ways of knowing what is going on around us and in the wider world. We need no longer "town criers" to keep us informed about the latest news. They have been replaced by reporters and journalists, who spread the news in the broad sense of the word "news."

Obviously, enormous power is found in mass communication. The people behind it somehow determine what to communicate and what not to communicate. Because they have such a wide variety of outlets and such a wide outreach, these people control our information and determine what we know and do not know.

Since almost unlimited abundance of information is available, there has to be someone, obviously, who selects what to communicate and what not to communicate. This is mainly done by reporters and journalists, too. When future reporters learn the art of journalism in school, the subject matter upon which they hone their skills is most often politics. In other words, most reporters are trained to be essentially political reporters, so their reporting often tends to take on a political tone. This can lead to severe distortions in coverage, especially in the area of reporting on religious matters. Even journalists who do report religious information are more trained in journalism than in the religion they write about.

Apparently, there is an enormous strength as well as an enormous weakness in mass communication. A person who was very much aware of both of these was Mary Angelica (1923-2016).

Mary Angelica, soon to be better known as Mother Angelica, was born Rita Antoinette Rizzo in Canton, Ohio, in a community of African-American and Italian immigrant mill workers. She had an Italian American background, the only child of John and Mae Helen Rizzo (born Gianfrancesco). Her father, a tailor by trade, abandoned the family when Rizzo was only five years old, and her parents divorced two years later. On March 10, 1931, her mother was granted custody of the young Rizzo, and her father was ordered to pay five dollars a week in child support, but according to Angelica, her mother only received "intermittent child-support payments from the father." While maintaining full custody, her mother struggled with chronic depression and poverty. This was in part because being a divorcée carried a social stigma at the time, and the opportunities for a woman to secure income were rather limited, especially in the height of the Great Depression.

Looking back at her childhood, Mother Angelica described herself and her mother as being "like a pair of refugees." As she said later, "We were poor, hungry, and barely surviving on odd jobs until Mother joined the dry cleaning business as an apprentice to a Jewish tailor in our area. Even then, we pinched pennies just to keep food on the table." The two lived with her maternal grandparents, moving out for a time between 1933 and 1937, but were forced to return because of financial pressures.

Rita Rizzo attended Canton McKinley High School, where she was one of the school's first drum majorettes. She later told an interviewer, "I did very poorly in school. I wasn't interested in the capital of Ohio. I was interested in whether my mother had committed suicide that day." Rizzo never dated, recalling later, "I never had a date, never wanted one. I just didn't have any desire. I suppose having experienced the worst of married life, it was not at all attractive to me."

A stomach ailment that Rita had from 1939 continued to cause her severe abdominal pain, despite the extensive medical treatment she received. Her mother took Rita to Rhoda Wise who was hailed as a mystic and stigmatic and who claimed to receive visions of Thérèse of Lisieux. Wise instructed Rizzo to do a novena (a nine-day course of prayers) and made the girl promise that she would spread devotion to the saint if she was cured.

On the novena's final day, January 18, 1943, Rita declared that she woke up with no pain, and the abdominal lump causing it had vanished. This experience profoundly touched her; she believed that God had performed a miracle, and she traced her lifelong commitment to God to this event. So she joined the Poor Clares, an order of cloistered contemplative nuns, officially called the Order of Saint Clare. She joined the order in Cleveland, Ohio. She was 21 years old when she was vested as a Poor Clare nun, and received a new name, "Sister Mary Angelica of the Annunciation."

In 1946, as a young nun, Sister Angelica had an accident with an industrial floor-scrubbing machine that knocked her over and injured her spine, causing her ongoing pain and requiring her to wear leg braces for most of her life. She saw the occurrence as a divine sign and promised Jesus, if she recovered, to build a new monastery deep in the Protestant-dominated Southern United States. She was ready to create a religious community which would appeal to African-Americans there.

In 1957, Archbishop Thomas Toolen suggested that she open this community in Birmingham. With a number of other Poor Clare nuns, she worked to raise the necessary funds, partially from a small business venture making and selling fishing lures. In 1961, the nuns bought a building and land, and in 1962, the community was officially established. It was located in Irondale, Alabama, and was named *Our Lady of the Angels Monastery*. Sister Angelica became now Mother Angelica.

After the nuns had made their new home in Irondale and funds were still desperately needed, the creation of the "Lil 'Ol Peanut Co." helped to keep the monastery running. However, this monastery would soon be relocated to Hanceville, Alabama, after Mother Angelica had visited Colombia where she claimed to have a vision which told her to build a temple in honor of the Child Jesus. Private donors contributed $48.6 million which allowed her to open the *Shrine of the Most Blessed Sacrament* in 1999.

It was still in 1962 that Mother Angelica had begun a series of community meetings on matters relevant to Catholicism, and also had started recording her talks for sale. That's when Bishop Joseph Vath noticed her talent for communicating with the lay public and encouraged her to continue. So she began taping a radio show for broadcast on Sunday mornings and published her first book in 1972. In the late 1970s she began videotaping her talks for television, which were broadcast on the satellite *Christian Broadcasting Network*.

3 Angelica, Mary: Mass Communication

In 1981, after visiting a Chicago television studio and being impressed by its capability, she founded the internationally broadcast cable television network *Eternal Word Television Network* (EWTN) and the radio network WEWN. Through these two networks, she made sure that her messages on the importance of Catholic identity would reach millions through EWTN and WEWN. Mother Angelica's live show endeared her to people from every walk of life. Her uncanny wit, down-to-earth humor, and ability to relate to the struggles of every-day existence proved to disarm the wary and enabled her to befriend the lonely.

EWTN became a voice for American conservative and traditional Catholics, with its position on religious and social issues often mirroring that of Pope John Paul II. Her start-up, EWTN, is credited with being the catalyst in the sudden increase in Catholic radio stations across America. Without EWTN, smaller networks could never have afforded to produce Catholic programming to fill a daily schedule. According to EWTN, the network's channels currently reach 264 million viewers in over 140 countries. The radio network, WEWN, is carried by 215 stations, as well as on shortwave. Mother Angelica's vision had been prophetic.

On Easter Sunday, 2016, Mother Angelica passed away. In a statement on EWTN's Facebook page, Father Sean O. Sheridan, then president of the Franciscan University of Steubenville—where Mother Angelica had received an honorary doctorate of sacred theology—described her as "a true media giant." She proved that the Church belonged in the popular media alongside the news, sports and talk shows. Though her stances were decidedly old-school—she was critical of religious and political progressives—her lectures were lightened with an often self-deprecating humor. She famously said the nuns she remembered from her youth were "the meanest people on God's earth."

Mother Angelica is another one of those Catholics who changed the world we live in. She made sure her network would report what no other network would: Catholicism. Without her, we would still be at the mercy of very opinionated journalists and highly selective media outlets.

4

Anselm of Canterbury: Slavery

We live in a world that is almost free of slavery. But that has not always been the case, as we all know. For centuries, slavery had been an accepted institution, in fact a universal human practice. The African slave trade was very much alive because slavery was very common in Africa, and slave trade had existed for centuries across the Sahara Desert to North Africa and the Middle East. Slave trade was carried out in great volume in the Middle Ages by the Arabs. Interestingly, the Muslim Kings of Mali, for instance, protested to the Amirs of Morocco that slave traders were seizing any black people when they were only supposed to seize non-Muslims. Sadly enough, there is currently an actual revival of slavery in Africa and the Middle East, where Boko Haram in Nigeria and ISIS in Syria and Iraq have been enslaving captives, including women who were raped and sold into sex slavery or forced marriages.

For centuries, slavery was a powerful economic system. In the earliest known records, we find slavery in any of its forms treated as an established institution. The Code of Hammurabi (c. 1760 BC), for example, prescribed death for anyone who helped a slave to escape or who sheltered a fugitive. We need to mention also that one important purpose of slavery in the

Ancient World was to discharge financial debts. There used to be no such thing as bankruptcy, or even a prison for debtors. People overwhelmed by debt would sell themselves into slavery. For less severe cases of debt, people might only have to sell their children. In the West and the East (especially China), the supply of prostitutes was usually made up by girls sold by their parents.

It is easy for us, at hindsight, to say that such practices are unacceptable. In the Ancient World, slavery was an economic and social cornerstone of society. Even the apostle Paul could not quite see how evil slavery is. The best he could say is that he himself had become a "slave" of Christ (Rom. 1:1). He even described Jesus as "taking the form of a slave" (Phil. 2:7). That may have taken the stigma of being a slave away, but not the evil of slavery itself. Paul did accept slavery in society, but he rejected the distinction between slaves and non-slaves within the Christian community. So Christians needed someone else to make them aware of the moral problem of slavery and slave trade. That person was Anselm of Canterbury (1033-1109).

Anselm is known for many things, but his opposition to slavery is not so well-known. In 1102, Anselm was able to have an ecclesiastical council pass a resolution against the British slave trade with the following decree: "Let no one dare hereafter to engage in the infamous business, prevalent in England, of selling men like animals." According to the Domesday Book census (1086), over 10% of England's population were slaves at the time. So Anselm was certainly forward-thinking at an era when slavery and slave trade were generally tolerated. But he was still too far ahead of his time, for this would not bolster the end of slavery itself. The council's resolution had no legislative powers, and no act of law was valid unless signed by the monarch anyway.

It would take much longer to entirely abolish slavery and slave trade—and it still exists in certain areas of the world. The US Constitution anticipated the abolition of the slave trade as early as 1808 and so did Great Britain. The British subsequently employed the Royal Navy to suppress all of the slave trade, over the protests of the Africans who were selling the slaves and of the Arabs who continued to trade in them.

Britain had already abolished slavery in its own country by way of case law, i.e. legal judgments that innocent persons could not be held in bondage in Great Britain. Then, in 1833, Britain abolished slavery in all its colonies. In the US, it took a great Civil War before Lincoln could finally abolish slavery. But it came at a huge price: it took at least 600,000 American lives in battle; by comparison, about 400,000 slaves had ever been imported into the country. The "battle" is still not over.

In spite of this long aftermath, Anselm had at least made his contemporaries aware of a moral problem that so many were blind to. Anselm saw in all clarity that the sale of human beings in the slave trade and the ownership of men and women in slavery are a violation of human dignity (§8) because a slave was regarded as no more than the property of someone else—as a thing rather than a person.

Anselm is another one of those Catholics who changed the world we live in. He made us aware what is wrong with a world tainted by slave trade and slavery.

5

Athanasius of Alexandria: One God

It is a common saying nowadays that there are three monotheistic religions—Judaism, Christianity and Islam. It's also said that all three of them worship the same God. If, according to monotheism, there can in principle only be one God, then Christians, Jews and Muslims must be worshipping the same God. So why then would we have three monotheistic religions instead of one? The answer is that Jesus made the difference. For Jews, he is a schismatic. For Muslims, he is a prophet, and nothing more. For Christians, he is the Son of God.

If this is true, if Jesus is indeed the Son of God in Christianity, then Christianity seems to be no longer a monotheistic religion. If God is really one, then there cannot be three of them: Father, Son and Holy Spirit. Either Christianity does not believe in one God, or it does really believe in one God, but then Jesus cannot be God. That's how the situation stands in the minds of many—not only nowadays, but as far back as the origin of Christianity.

The idea that Jesus cannot be God became very popular in Christianity through the influence of *Arianism*. Beginning in 313, Arius had been building quite a following in one of the most prestigious churches in Egypt, which was given to him by

5 Athanasius of Alexandria: One God

bishop Alexander of Alexandria, of all people. His message seemed indeed quite orthodox—God is one—but then he veered off in an unorthodox direction—if God is one, then Jesus can't be God as well. He admitted that Jesus is the incarnation of the Word, directly created by God. However, God made the Word first, out of nothing, so that he could use him to create everything else, according to Arius. Since the Son was created out of nothing, like everything else, there obviously was a time when the Son was *not*. If the Father begot the Son, then he that was begotten must have had a beginning of existence. So there had to be a time when the Son was not the Son. He had to be created at some point in time. In short, Jesus is not God as far as Arians are concerned.

Arianism appears so clear, simple and logical that it becomes very attractive. First it assumes that Jesus really is a son in the regular sense, by insisting that no son is as old as his own father. But then it turns things around by using this premise to conclude that Jesus is no son at all, except in an analogous way. From there, it makes tiny, but persuading logical steps: if Jesus is Son, then he was begotten; if he is begotten, then he had a beginning; if he had a beginning, then he is not infinite; if he is not infinite, then he is not God. It is as simple as one plus one is two—at least that's how it appears to be!

This way, Arians made Christianity more acceptable for monotheistic believers by reducing it to a mere variant of Judaism and Islam: there is only one God (§19). Although many people nowadays believe this still to be true, Christianity has vehemently rejected this claim as a heresy. There is indeed only one God, but it is a triune God—Father, Son and Holy Spirit. Jesus is God who became Man—God-made-flesh, the God-Man, which means Jesus is in fact *God* (but you cannot reverse it, for God is not Jesus). Father and Son are two in name, but they are one God, not two Gods. This is the orthodoxy of Christianity. One of the strongest defenders of orthodoxy in Christianity was Athanasius of Alexandria (296-373).

His voice was very prominent at the Council of Nicaea in 325, where Arianism was nailed. What had never been done before by a Council was that the attending bishops—between 250 and 300—expressed orthodox Church teaching by drafting a Creed that all were bound to accept: the so-called Nicene Creed.

How could Athanasius be the staunch defender of the Nicene Creed? Athanasius was certainly not impressive, with his short, delicate stature. Later, the hostile Emperor Julian, better known as "Julian the Apostate," would call him a "black dwarf." But where the ancient, orthodox Faith was concerned, he was obstinate, intransigent and stubborn as a donkey. After Athanasius had left the desert and became secretary to Alexander, the patriarch of Alexandria, he brought with him a book that he had written—*On the Incarnation,* which would now be officially published. C. S. Lewis (§0) would later praise it for the "classical simplicity" of its style. The book is addressed to a recent convert named Macarius, who had heard some confusing objections made against the deity of Christ, probably of Arian origin. It contains many jewels of orthodox Christian doctrine.

In this book, Athanasius made it crystal clear that Jesus was truly God and truly man, both Son of God and Son of man, the God-Man. He came down from Heaven, God from God, light from light, taking on a human form to become our Savior. There are many masterful insights in his masterpiece *On the Incarnation,* showing us how sound, solid, and clear Athanasius' teachings are, and how much they were in defiance

5 Athanasius of Alexandria: One God

of Arianism. Athanasius saw clearly that the deity of Christ is actually the cornerstone of our salvation—without it, everything would fall apart. If Christ were only a human creature, the Gospel would not truly be such good news after all. Creation can only be renewed or restored by its Creator. Therefore, the Son of God, the God-Man Jesus, came to be among sinners and came to die so that we might live. Only God can do that! If Jesus is not God, then our salvation is a hoax.

The question still remained for many Christians how God, the eternal and immortal one, could ever get involved with human flesh. Did the flesh of the Son of man deprive him from his divinity as the Son of God? Athanasius vehemently rejected this old fallacy. By doing so, Athanasius became a champion of the Nicene cause. He was a tireless defender of Trinitarianism, and therefore, an unwavering foe of the Arians. For good reason, he became known as "Athanasius against the World." In the Eastern Orthodox Church, he is labeled as the "Father of Orthodoxy." Some Protestant groups call him "Father of the Canon." It was his aim to eradicate Arianism from the face of the earth. Without him, all Christians could have become Arians.

But Arianism did not die that easily. Even when the Nicene Council had ended, the fight was far from over for Athanasius. After Nicaea, emperors—both Emperor Constantine (§19) and his successors—would periodically recant their support for Christian orthodoxy and go back and forth in their official support for Arianism. One could easily say that Arianism was most of the time a state-sponsored heresy. Yet, each time they enforced Arianism again, the emperors had Athanasius battling against them. His opposition to Arianism caused him to be expelled from his see in Alexandria five times, but he regained it each time. After long years of fight and flight, he was restored to his see in Alexandria, where he spent seven peaceful years until his death in 373.

But don't think Arianism is something of the past now. It is still alive in some form today—not only inside Christianity in branches such as Unitarianism, but also outside Christianity in a religion such as Islam, which only emerged a few centuries later while Arianism was still very much alive and popular. Although Mohammed lived three centuries after the Nicene Creed, we shouldn't forget that the Christians Mohammed knew were still Arians, or had at least been affected by Arian doctrines. One of the first times we hear about the link between Islam and Arianism is in the writings of a later Church Father John of Damascus (675-749). He was convinced that Islam was in essence not a separate religion, but instead a heretical form of Christianity. The late historian Hilaire Belloc echoed the same idea about Islam—that it "was essentially in its origins not a new religion, but a heresy." Although Mohammed did not learn much from Christianity, he did get the gist of Arianism: Jesus is not God. Not surprisingly, the areas of the Roman Empire where Arianism had been very popular were now wide open to Islam.

This puts a different light on the claim that Christianity and Islam are both monotheistic religions that worship the same God. What Alexander had made undeniably clear is that they are not worshipping the same God. The Christian God is a "triune" God—not three Gods, but one God in three persons: Father, Son and Holy Spirit. That's certainly not so in Islam. So we should ask the question, as was done in the title of a recent book, "Is the Father of Jesus the God of Mohammed?" Or are they essentially different instead? Even the Qur'an itself suggests that the God of the Qur'an is radically different from the God Christians worship. The Qur'an specifically tells us that

5 Athanasius of Alexandria: One God

Christ was not divine, was not crucified, and that belief in the Trinity is polytheism. To affirm these teachings constitutes blasphemy for Muslims. That makes it hard to claim that Allah is the same God as the Christian God.

Athanasius may have won the battle against Arianism in Christianity, but Arian ideas seem to have survived outside of Christianity—and they seem to have come back in modern times because Arianism appears so logical and attractive. Many people nowadays consider Jesus merely a great *man*. Religions such as Mormonism and Islam are effectively Arian in theology. The explanations of Athanasius, on the other hand, are much more complicated and require more than a simple "formula." Athanasius made sure that Christianity is a monotheistic religion, but at the same time he made sure we don't simplify its monotheism.

Athanasius is another one of those Catholics who changed the world we live in. Without Athanasius, all Christians in the world could very well be Arians, and no longer Christians.

6

Barat, Madeleine-Sophie: Education of Women

We are so used to equal education for boys and girls that it's hard to believe how for centuries education was mainly given to half the population—to the male part, that is (§2)—but education for young women and girls was hardly available at the time. For changing this "tradition," we have to thank Madeleine-Sophie Barat (1779-1865).

Madeleine-Sophie grew up in a financially comfortable family whose ancestors had lived in Joigny for generations and were proud of their roots in Burgundy. Her father, Jacques Barat was a cooper and vine-grower. Both professions were respected trades, with centuries of French culture and spirituality behind them. The Barats were Jansenist Catholics, and Jansenism is often said to have shaped Sophie's spirituality profoundly.

Louis, Madeleine-Sophie's older brother, became a teacher of mathematics at his old school and decided to take on Sophie's education. He "home-schooled" her with Latin, Greek, history, natural science, Spanish and Italian, thus providing Sophie with an education rarely available to young women and girls at that time.

She went to Paris in 1795, at the height of the French Revolution, and initially considered becoming a Carmelite nun. However, her experience of Revolutionary violence in France led her on another path. In 1800, she founded the *Society of the Sacred Heart* whose purpose was to make known the love of God revealed in the Heart of Christ and take part in the restoration of Christian life in France through the education of young women of the rich and the poor classes.

The first school was opened in Amiens in northern France in September 1801, and Sophie traveled to this important provincial city in order to teach. Sophie made her vows on June 7, 1802. The new community and school grew quickly. A school giving classes to poor girls of the town was opened next. In December 1802, at the age of twenty-three, Sophie became Superior of the Society.

The *Society of the Sacred Heart* quickly expanded within Europe and beyond. In November, 1804, Sophie traveled to Sainte-Marie-d'en-Haut, near Grenoble in southeastern France, to receive a community of Visitation nuns into the Society. Among them was Philippine Duchesne, who would later introduce the Society to America. A second school was then established at Grenoble, followed by a third at Poitiers in western France. After these first establishments in France, foundations were established in North America (1818), Italy (1828), Switzerland (1830), Belgium (1834), Algiers (1841), England (1842), Ireland (1842), Spain (1846), Holland (1848), Germany (1851), South America (1853), Austria (1853), and Poland (1857).

In 1820, Madeleine called all the superiors together in a council at Paris in order to establish a uniform course of studies for the quickly expanding network of Sacred Heart schools.

These studies were to be serious, to cultivate the mind, and to create young women who would be devoted to the Sacred Heart of Jesus and perform good deeds in God's name. The Sacred Heart schools quickly earned an excellent reputation. Madeleine dreamed of educating all girls regardless of their parents' financial means. For almost every new school established, a corresponding "free" school was opened to provide the poorer girls of the area with a high-quality education that they would not otherwise have received. It was by her awareness of their impact on the world of education that she ensured the Society's contribution to the education and the promotion of women in her time and into the future.

In her own words,

> "How rare it is to find a valiant woman! ... Let is work to train a few. For in this century we must no longer count on men to preserve the faith. The grain of faith that will be saved will hide itself among women. A woman cannot remain neutral in the world. She too is set for the fall and resurrection of many."

Madeleine Sophie Barat is another one of those Catholics who changed the world we live in. She introduced to the world the education of girls and women that we consider so normal nowadays. By the time of her death in Paris on May 25, 1865, she had opened more than 100 houses and schools in twelve countries, institutions known for the quality of the education made available to young women.

7

Bede the Venerable: History

When talking about the past, we basically talk history. History is something we learn in school, something we study to compose reports and statistics, something we watch on the History Channel, and something telling us how we came to the point where we are now. History seems to be the best example of dealing with the facts we want to know about the past.

How did we come to this conception? How do we know that the century we live in is in fact the "twenty-first" century? It is probably much more than following your gut feelings. Someone must have informed us this way. That "someone" must have been a historian. Well, there are many historians nowadays. But one that sticks out in the crowd is Bede the Venerable (672-735).

Bede was given to the monks of Wearmouth-Jarrow Abby in England when he was only seven years old. He never left. In his own words, "From that time, I have spent the whole of my life within that monastery, devoting all my pains to the study of the Scriptures, and amid the observance of monastic discipline and the daily charge of singing in the church, it has ever been my delight to learn or teach or write." And learning and teaching and writing he did. He was deeply versed in all the sciences of his times: astronomy, arithmetic, grammar, and, especially, Holy Scripture. But what he has become best known for is *history*.

Bede is remembered today as the earliest historian whose work has shed light on a period of English history that would have otherwise been unknown. His most famous work, *Ecclesiastical History of the English People*, gained him the title "The Father of English History." It is an account of Britain between the landings of Julius Caesar in 55/54 BC and Augustine of Canterbury in AD 597.

Bede's thoroughness and accuracy are the book's strengths, and considering the limitations of the day, his achievement is remarkable: he quoted some 144 separate works, and no doubt, consulted even more. He asked traveling monks to consult Vatican archives for him, and he used many witnesses scattered over Europe. Fortunately, the monastery at Wearmouth-Jarrow itself had an excellent library. It has been estimated that there were about 200 books in the monastic library, which was enormous for the 7th century.

Bede ranks not only as the first English historian, but also as one of the best. His *Ecclesiastical History* is commonly regarded as of decisive importance in the art and science of writing history. In an age where little was attempted beyond the registration of "facts," he had reached the conception of "history," which is more than a collection of facts. No wonder, one recent historian described him as "the first and greatest of England's historians." Another one said of him that he "holds a privileged and unrivalled place among first historians of Christian Europe."

Besides, it needs to be noted that he wrote the first work of history in which the AD system of dating is used. The terms *Anno Domini* (AD) and *Before Christ* (BC) are still being used

7 Bede the Venerable: History

to label or number years in the Julian and Gregorian calendars (§33). The term *Anno Domini* means "in the year of the Lord." This calendar scheme is based on the traditionally reckoned year of the conception or birth of Jesus of Nazareth, with AD counting years from the start of this epoch, and BC denoting years before the start of the era. There is no year zero in this scheme, so the year AD 1 immediately follows the year 1 BC. This dating system was already devised in 525, but was not widely used until Bede widely promoted it.

Bede did much more than writing history. He also knew, for instance, that the world was not flat and that the moon affected the tides. He also wrote extensively on other issues. He was a teacher, besides. For example, one of his students, Alcuin (§2), went on to become an influential figure in the court of Charlemagne. Bede's writings were filled with such faith and learning that even while he was still alive, a Church council ordered them to be read publicly in the churches. As his reputation spread, various kings and even popes desired his presence as a scholar-in-residence. Yet, except for a few months, Bede remained in the monastery of Jarrow until his death. Nevertheless, his fame spread over all of the Western world. In 1899, Pope Leo XIII declared him a Doctor of the Church. He is the only native of Great Britain to achieve this designation.

Bede is another one of those Catholics who changed the world we live in. It may not have been the world itself he changed, but the way we see the world and write about its past.

8

Bellarmine, Robert: Human Rights

The term "Human Rights" is a buzzword everywhere nowadays! It is even in the air we breathe in daily. We hear about it in the news media, it is used in demonstrations, on billboards, in speeches, in Congress, in political parties, and the list goes on and on. What is the "buzz" about? It's about *rights*! We have the right to be free; we have the right to vote; we have the right of free speech; we have the right to life; we have the right to follow our conscience; we have the right to abortion; we have the right to do as one pleases—and again, the list goes on and on. Every mouth is full of "rights" which we think we have the "right" to defend.

Some people think of human rights as if they were entitlements that the government gives us. Indeed, we gain entitlements as we age—in the USA, we can drive a car at sixteen, vote at eighteen, and buy alcohol at twenty-one. But we cannot just apply this kind of reasoning to human rights. Entitlements we only have because we belong to a certain society, whereas rights we have because we are part of the human family. The government can hand out entitlements, but it cannot give rights away, although it may sometimes try to take them away.

8 Bellarmine, Robert: Human Rights

Where does all this talk about "rights" come from? You might think it comes from the United Nations. Indeed, in 1948, the UN affirmed in its *Universal Declaration of Human Rights* that "all human beings are born free and equal in dignity and rights." But what does that mean? The Declaration famously left the term "right" vague in order to achieve passage. The Catholic philosopher Jacques Maritain (§46) said, paradoxically, "We agree on these rights, on condition that no one asks us why."

You might also think, like many in the USA do, that the origin of the term "rights" can be found much earlier: in the *US Declaration of Independence*, drafted by Thomas Jefferson in 1776, declaring that we are endowed by our Creator with certain unalienable rights. Unlike the UN declaration, the US Declaration makes at least clear where these rights come from: the only reason we have human rights is that God endows us with rights—they are God-given, not man-made.

So the answer might be that talking about rights finds its origin in the USA. In a sense, that is true, but it is not the entire or best answer. One of its drafters, Jefferson, had been inspired by—or at least had read about—someone else some two centuries earlier: Robert Bellarmine (1542–1621). Who is Bellarmine?

Bellarmine's early intellectual accomplishments had given his father hope that Bellarmine would restore the family's fortunes through a political career. However, his mother's wish that he enter the Society of Jesus prevailed. On completion of his studies as a Jesuit, Bellarmine taught first at the University of Louvain in Belgium. In 1576, he accepted the invitation of Pope Gregory XIII to teach theology at the new Roman College, now known as the Pontifical Gregorian University. Robert Bellarmine spent the next eleven years teaching and writing a three-volume defense of the Catholic faith against the arguments of the Protestant Reformers. In 1597, Pope Clement VIII made him his own theologian. Then, in 1599, he made him Cardinal, alleging as his reason for this promotion that "the Church of God had not his equal in learning."

What does this Bellarmine have to do with human rights? When we read the writings of Robert Bellarmine, such as his treatise on civil government (*De Laicis*), we find there, "All men are equal, not in wisdom or grace, but in the essence and nature of mankind." That sounds familiar! Besides, Bellarmine also dealt with the same issue that the new government in the US had to deal with: what kind of government do we want? On this issue, he made some clear statements: "There is no reason why among equals one should rule rather than another.... Let rulers remember that they preside over men who are of the same nature as they themselves." Considering the origins of political power, Bellarmine wrote, "Political power emanates from God. Government was introduced by divine law, but the divine law has given this power to no particular man.... It depends upon the consent of the multitude to constitute over itself a king, consul, or other magistrate."

Even if these words of Bellarmine do sound familiar to US ears, this does not prove that Jefferson had read them. Yet, there is a clear indication that he had read them indirectly. Jefferson had in his personal library (preserved in the Library of Congress) a well-read and heavily annotated copy of *Patriarcha*, written by the anti-Catholic Protestant Robert Filmer, who had been the court theologian to King James I of England, and who was fiercely vigilant against any threat to the divine right of kings. Filmer heavily focused in his book on Bellarmine's idea of popular sovereignty, and of course, rejected it as a threat to the king. Yet, even a casual reading of

8 Bellarmine, Robert: Human Rights

the text by Jefferson would have placed Bellarmine's thought squarely before him.

How did Bellarmine come up with his thoughts on human rights? In fact, his thinking was profoundly grounded in the teachings of the Church, most notably of Thomas Aquinas (§60). This "Angelic Doctor" made huge contributions to the Catholic teaching on the human person and on human rights. In doing so, Bellarmine was just a powerful spokesman for the Church's eternally valuable insights into the human condition. If, then, Jefferson was indeed influenced by Bellarmine, the author of the Declaration was also shaped by Aquinas and the whole of the Catholic intellectual tradition. And so, too, was the form of government chosen by its Founding Fathers.

But nevertheless, it was Bellarmine who spread this deep insight into the wider world, including the New World. He argued that kings do not rule by divine right, but through the consent of the governed people. Although all power comes from God, each nation is a political unit composed of individual souls that are by their nature free and equal creations of God. Being free and equal, none has any more or less right to rule than another. This was certainly a radical idea in the early 1600's, though it became more accepted two centuries later, and is widely accepted today.

This idea should not have been so radical because it had always been part of Catholic Social Teaching (§44)—the hidden jewel of the Catholic Church. It finds its grounding in the fact that God has loved us, continues to love us, and will always love us—so nothing can remove that love. This is often called the Dignity of Human life; all human life is sacred since God loves all. Every human person therefore is born with innate rights and dignity, retaining that dignity from conception to natural death. It does not matter how we choose to live our lives; each life has a dignity that must be respected. And Robert Bellarmine was a strong ambassador for this classical social teaching of the Church. He made it ultimately spread as far as the New World.

But Bellarmine did much more for this world. Regardless of all his intellectual achievements, Bellarmine had a very human face. He gave most of his money to the poor. Once he gave the tapestries from his living quarters to the poor, saying that the walls wouldn't catch cold. It was discovered at his death in 1621 that he had quietly given away all his money; there was not even enough left to pay for his funeral. Those were practical consequences of his belief in human equality and human rights.

It should not surprise us then that Cardinal Avery Dulles, S.J., said about Bellarmine: "About the time that I became a Catholic, in my first semester of Harvard Law School, I devoured James Brodrick's two-volume life of Bellarmine and came to admire the saint's many-sided personality and his manifold accomplishments." Bellarmine's plea for human rights and human dignity is only a small part of it. When asked to choose a confirmation name after his conversion to Catholicism, Dulles selected without hesitation "Robert," the first name of Cardinal Bellarmine.

Bellarmine is another one of those Catholics who changed the world we live in. It may have taken a while, but nowadays most people would agree with the thoughts he had about human rights and human dignity as early as the 1600s.

9

Benedict of Nursia: Hospitals

If you know of people in your surroundings or in your circle of friends and relatives who have never been in a hospital, for themselves or others, you are pretty unique. Hospitals are part of life these days because sickness, diseases and injuries are part of life too. Many people nowadays were even born in a hospital, and when they die, it's often also in a hospital. But that hasn't always been that way. Diseases may have always been part of the human condition, but hospitals were not. Yet, today, we could certainly wonder where many of us would be without hospitals.

Of course, there have probably always been witchdoctors, sorcerers and shamans, but hospitals are a much more recent invention. Gradually, some kind of medical profession did develop in the Roman Empire, but it was of a rather primitive nature. Besides, medical care was basically only for the wealthy who could afford it. Although the Romans did have some kind of field hospitals for the treatment of their sick and injured soldiers, the only purpose of those places was to keep the military power of ancient Rome operational. The Romans lacked belief in charity and in human dignity. Therefore, it would require the work of someone else to start hospitals for everyone—rich or poor, young or old. To find that person, we need to go back to the early Middle Ages in Europe, back to Benedict of Nursia (480-543).

Benedict is probably best known as the founder of many Benedictine monasteries. But what many people don't realize is that most of those monasteries used to be associated with hospitals—actually the first ones in Europe during the Middle Ages. Here is how it began, thanks to Benedict.

Benedict was a devout Italian Christian who became a monk at the age of 20, wishing to withdraw from the world after he visited Rome and was shocked by how immoral life in the Holy City had become. After this experience, he left Rome and founded his own monastery in 529 in Subiaco, some fifty miles to the east of Rome. Soon he would found 12 more monasteries in the vicinity of Subiaco, and eventually, in 530, he founded the great Benedictine monastery of Monte Cassino, which lies on a hilltop between Rome and Naples. The monastery remained there until it was almost completely destroyed in a series of heavy American-led air raids at the end of World War II. The bombing was conducted because many reports from the British commanders on the ground suggested that Germans were occupying the monastery, which turned out not to be true. The Abbey was rebuilt after the war and re-consecrated in 1964.

It is in this monastery of Monte Cassino that Benedict founded a hospital that is considered today to have been the first hospital in Europe of the new era. It was there that Benedictine monks took care of the sick and wounded according to Benedict's Rule. The monastic routine called for hard work. The care of the sick was hard work and of such importance that those caring for them were told to act as if they were serving Christ directly.

The same was done at the other twelve monasteries near

Subiaco. Hospitals were settled as adjuncts to the monasteries also in order to provide charity and care for soldiers and patients. Since that time the Benedictines were very involved in healing and caring for the sick and dying, so in many cases early Medieval medicine was closely connected with Christianity and the Benedictines in particular. This is the reason why very often the early Middle Ages are called "the Benedictine centuries."

In the 6th–12th centuries, the Benedictines established lots of monk communities of this type. In the many monasteries that were founded throughout Europe, everywhere there were hospitals like in Monte Cassino. During the 10th century, the monasteries became a dominant factor in hospital work. The famous Benedictine Abbey of Cluny, founded in 910, set the example which was widely imitated throughout France and Germany. Besides its infirmary for the religious, each monastery had a hospital in which other patients were cared for.

By the 11th century, some monasteries were training their own physicians. Ideally, such physicians would uphold the Christianized ideal of the healer who offered mercy and charity towards all patients and soldiers, whatever their status and prognosis might be. And later, in the 12th–13th centuries, the Benedictine Order built a network of independent hospitals, initially to provide general care to the sick and wounded, and then for treatment of syphilis and isolation of patients with contagious diseases. The hospital movement spread through Europe in the subsequent centuries, with a 225-bed hospital being built at York, England in 1287, and even larger facilities established at Florence, Paris, Milan, Siena and other medieval big European cities.

In general, it could be said that medieval hospitals in Europe were religious communities, with care provided by monks and nuns. Let's not forget that an old French term for hospital is *hôtel-Dieu*, "hostel of God." That's a rather appropriate term given the fact that many hospitals were attached to monasteries. The link with monasteries remained for a while. In this period, hospitals preserved both the symbolic and material link to the Church and religion based on the idea that the body and the soul were closely connected and mutually affected. That link was so strong that physicians refused to treat patients who had not made a confession, as the sacrament of confession purified the soul from sins.

No wonder, then, hospitals frequently resembled monasteries. Patients were occasionally required to follow the monastic rules, and some hospitals admitted 12 male patients in an obvious reference to the 12 apostles. Even the hospital architecture was supposed to inspire religious devotion—the leading European hospital, the Florentine Santa Maria della Nuova, had a cross-shaped ground-plan, with the long axis serving as the male and the short as the female ward. The monastery-like hospital interior included frescoes with Biblical motives and altars adorned with Christian iconography.

In the meantime, there was another development taking place: the start of the crusades in the 11th century. Hospitals flourished during the crusades, with the rise of orders specialized for that service, such as the Hospitaller Knights. But, by the 13th century, growing urban communities had taken over the leading cultural role from monasteries. When monastic hospitals and hospital orders, such as the energetic Sisters of Mercy, continued to grow, hospitals physically and administratively moved to the cities.

In Europe, after the seeds had been planted by Benedict, the medieval concept of Christian care evolved during the sixteenth and seventeenth centuries into a more secular one. But there was a problem lurking. The Protestant Reformers rejected the Catholic belief that rich men could gain God's grace through good works—and thus escape purgatory—by providing endowments to charitable institutions, and that the patients themselves could gain grace through their suffering.

In lands such as France, where Protestants had not gained much traction, rich families continued to fund convents and monasteries that provided free health care services to the poor. French practices were influenced by a charitable imperative which considered care of the poor and the sick to be a necessary part of Catholic practice. The nursing nuns had little faith in the power of physicians and their medicines alone to cure the sick; more important was providing psychological and physical comfort, nourishment, rest, cleanliness and especially prayer.

In Protestant areas, on the other hand, the emphasis was on professional rather than religious aspects of patient care, and this helped develop a view of health care as a profession rather than a vocation. As a consequence, in the mainly Protestant countries after 1530, there was little hospital development. Some smaller groups such as the Moravians and the Pietists saw a role for hospitals, especially in their missionary work, but that was rather exceptional. Benedict's inspiration was gradually losing its power there. But his vital role in health care remains undeniable.

Benedict of Nursia is another one of those Catholics who changed the world we live in. The seeds for our health care system were planted by him. It is hard to tell what this system would look like nowadays without his impact.

10

Bosco, Giovanni: Urbanization

Cities have many advantages that attract people, but they also create their own problems. Urbanization—the shift from rural to urban areas—comes at a high cost: unemployment, broken families, homeless people, abandoned children, street gangs and so much more that is particularly harmful to the youngest generation. Urbanization doesn't only occur in developed countries but in developmental countries, too, where the trek to cities also creates more problems than it solves. In francophone countries, such towns are referred to as *bidonvilles* (French for "can town"), built of oil drums or other metal containers, especially arising on the outskirts of many African cities. One could say that cities are, in some sense, deserts for human beings.

Someone who saw what urbanization can do to the youngest generation growing up in the cities was Giovanni Bosco, better known as John Bosco or Don Bosco (1815-1888).

While working in Turin, he saw with his very own eyes how the population suffered many of the effects of industrialization and urbanization: numerous poor families lived in the slums of the city, having come from the countryside in search of a better life. When visiting the prisons, Don Bosco was disturbed to see there so many boys from 12 to 18 years of age. He was determined to find a means to prevent them from ending up in those places. So he decided to dedicate his life to the betterment and education of street children, juvenile delinquents and other disadvantaged youth.

So what did he do? He educated them! What made Bosco's dream so revolutionary is that he taught "his boys" how to make a living—not with begging or food stamps but with education, so they wouldn't end up on the streets, in gangs, or in prison. He did so by developing new teaching methods. They were based on love rather than punishment, a method that became known as the Salesian Preventive System. Punishment was not in Don Bosco's vocabulary. Observance of rules was obtained by instilling a true sense of duty, by removing all occasions for disobedience and by making sure no effort towards virtue would pass unappreciated. He held that the teacher should be father, adviser and friend—all based on the preventive method instead of punishment. Of punishment he said: "As far as possible avoid punishing… [and] try to gain love before inspiring fear." His "dream" was basically simple—to prevent a person from becoming bad.

Probably the most innovative part of his work was finding jobs for them as apprentices. This way he helped thousands of disadvantaged youth. He put together ground-breaking contracts of apprenticeship. All of them had to be signed by the employer, the apprentice, and Don Bosco himself. In those contracts, Don Bosco touched on many sensitive issues. Some employers customarily used apprentices as their servants, so Don Bosco obliged them to agree to employ the boys only in their acknowledged trade. Since employers also used to beat the boys, Don Bosco required them to agree that corrections be made only verbally. He cared for their health, and therefore demanded that they be given a fair pay, rest on feast days, and that they be given an annual holiday.

All in all, John Bosco was a visionary who saw what the world needed: a better future for the young generation, especially the most disadvantaged ones. His vision spread like wildfire. He dedicated his works to Francis De Sales when he founded the *Salesians of Don Bosco*, based in Turin. Together with Maria Mazzarello, he founded the *Institute of the Daughters of Mary Help of Christians*, a religious congregation of nuns dedicated to the care and education of poor girls.

Indeed, he was a "dreamer," but a dreamer who lived with both feet on the ground. He wasn't a dreamer who just dreams, but one who makes his dreams come true. He even had an incredible vision in 1883, showing him that his people would travel to the ends of the earth via automobiles, freeways and airplanes, long before they existed! His dream has come true, as now there are about 2,000 Salesian communities in 130 countries all over the globe, using cars, freeways and airplanes.

Of course, Don Bosco was not the only one to see this need in our cities. Other Catholics would follow his example. In 1917, Fr. Edward J. Flanagan founded *Boys Town*, which has now 12 regional headquarters in the USA. And there are many organizations nowadays all over the world that claim to be inspired by Don Bosco. That's what a "dreamer" can do!

Don Bosco is another one of those Catholics who changed the world we live in. He saw what urbanization does to the youngest generation, and he showed us what to do about its harmful effects.

11

Brandsma, Titus: Freedom of Press

A contentious issue in our society is "freedom of expression," and by extension, "freedom of the press." If we can't say what we want or if we can't write what we want, then we feel suppressed by our government, by our Church, or whatever institution is presumably suppressing us. Freedom is something very dear to us—something many want to defend, and sometimes are even willing to die for.

Perhaps a bit more needs to be said on this issue. Is this freedom unlimited? Should we really be free and allowed to say or write *whatever* we want? Usually this idea is further qualified by saying that we should be free to express or write the truth, *whatever* the truth is—as long as it is the truth and nothing but the truth, no matter what that truth is. This was at least the opinion and conviction of Titus Brandsma (1881-1942). Who was he?

In September 1898, Anno Brandsma presented himself at a Carmelite monastery in Holland, as a candidate for the order. He was gladly accepted. On entering the novitiate, he observed the custom of changing his name to indicate the beginning of his new life. His choice was Titus, the one who battled corrupt teachings. After further studies, Brandsma became a professor of philosophy and the history of mysticism at the Catholic University of Nijmegen in 1923.

An important turn in his life came when Nazi Germany was on the rise. Brandsma began to realize the dangers of national-socialism before anyone else and warned the people about it. As early as 1933, when Hitler became Chancellor of Germany, Brandsma was already criticizing his racial policies towards the Jews. In 1936, Brandsma openly expressed his serious concern about a certain lack of militancy, enthusiasm and spirit of sacrifice among Catholic journalists. Brandsma put the pressure of the circumstances of the times on the journalists and on journalism in general. Titus, with sadness and foreboding, observed and correctly interpreted the ominous development of Nazism. In classroom, lecture halls and the press, he warned the Dutch against Hitler's tyranny. "The Nazi movement is a black lie," he proclaimed. "It is pagan." He saw it as a definite threat to freedom of expression, more in particular, freedom of the press.

Then, in 1935, the ranking prelate of Holland, Archbishop (later Cardinal) de Jong of Utrecht appointed Brandsma chaplain to the flourishing Catholic press in the country; there were over 30 Catholic daily newspapers in the Netherlands at the time, with three of them having a national readership. Although he was not a professional journalist himself, he was a natural for the job: he was a professor of Philosophy and was also a prolific writer, who had been contributing articles to over 80 different publications. He was a frequent guest on radio programs and travelled throughout the Netherlands and beyond, delivering lectures on various subjects. One of his students humorously noted that Fr. Titus was the only mystic he knew who had a season ticket railway pass!

On May 10, 1940, German tanks bearing the swastika and

flying red war banners burst across the Dutch border, spearheading a blitzkrieg that rapidly crushed all organized military resistance. The Dutch bishops reacted swiftly. They announced on January 26, 1941, that the Sacraments were to be refused to Catholics of whom it was known that they were supporting the National-Socialist movement to a considerable extent. After release of the bishops' letter, the military governor of Holland declared open war on the Dutch Catholics in a speech delivered in Amsterdam: "From this moment on it will be either you are with us or against us. The struggle will not be over until everyone accepts the way we, the Nazis, want things to be done."

Following the Nazi invasion of the Netherlands, the Nazi forces began also constantly testing the mentality of the journalists and the directors of journals. With armed forces in command and Nazi officials and collaborators in political control, the repression of freedom, including the freedom of the press, became the objective in Holland. In response, through a letter addressed to the Dutch people in July 1941, the bishops declared openly, "Our Catholic daily press has either been suspended or has been so limited in its freedom of expression that it is hardly possible any longer to speak of a Catholic Press."

At the end of 1941 and the beginning of 1942, the journals were forced to publish Nazi propaganda. Freedom of the press had come under even more serious attack! The Nazi public relations bureau informed Dutch newspapers and journals that they had to accept advertisements and press releases emanating from official sources. In an official publication of January 16, 1942, the bishops, after advice from Brandsma, prohibited not only controversial propaganda, but also the publication of the articles from the "editorial board" which could be interpreted as favorable towards the National-Socialist Movement.

Shortly after issuance of this memorandum, Archbishop de Jong summoned Titus to his chancery and told him, "We will respond to them. Our answer must be 'No!'" He commissioned Titus, in his capacity as spiritual director of Catholic journalists, to convey the hierarchy's response personally to all Catholic editors in the Netherlands. On presenting this task, the archbishop said: "Titus, you do understand this mission is dangerous. You do not have to undertake it."

Without any hesitation, in January 1942, Brandsma visited all the Dutch Catholic journals to deliver by hand a letter from the Conference of Dutch Bishops to the editors of Catholic newspapers in which the bishops ordered them not to print official Nazi documents, although required under a new law by the German occupiers. It was clearly stated why they should not publish the advertisements coming from the Germans. Newspapers that did not follow this episcopal order would no longer be allowed to call themselves Catholic. Brandsma personally encouraged the editors to resist Nazi demands while patiently explaining the various consequences of such resistance as well as of collaboration with occupation authorities. He concluded each visit with remarks along this line: "Our limit has been reached! We cannot serve them!" The Carmelite Dutch priest courageously told the journalists in Holland, in no uncertain terms, "We will not do it!"

This Carmelite Priest knew that the reprisals against him would be severe. He knew he would dearly pay for this. He did not think, though, that they would be so swift; within days he was arrested. Brandsma had only visited 14 editors before the Gestapo arrested him on Monday, January 19, 1942, at 6 p.m. at his monastery.

11 Brandsma, Titus: Freedom of Press

It was his resolute and well-reflected performance as spiritual adviser of the Catholic journalist and publishers that became the cause for his detention in his monastery in the Netherlands. And six months later, he died at the age of 61 at the Dachau concentration camp, a martyr for the cause of freedom of the press. He died from a lethal injection administered by a nurse of the SS, as part of their program of medical experimentation on the prisoners.

Brandsma paid dearly, with his own life, for defending the freedom of the press. Though not a journalist himself in the strict sense, Brandsma is considered in press circles a martyr for the freedom of the press. In 1992, the *Titus Brandsma Award* was conferred for the first time at the UCIP world congress in Brazil. This Award is one of the most prestigious in the world of the media, honoring journalists, publishers, professors of communication, publications or institutes who have suffered threats or persecution because of their engagement in the media on behalf of an important humanitarian or Christian issue.

The award is an on-going call, in the spirit of Titus Brandsma, for journalists to take their profession seriously in the most bizarre circumstances. It is also a call to all men and women in journalism to keep alive the idea of justice in the media and to bring justice to today's world. In contrast, keeping silence in the face of injustice would only destroy the fundamentals of their profession.

The bottom line is undeniable. Titus Brandsma was imprisoned by the German Nazis for encouraging the Catholic press in the Netherlands not to bend to the will and the ideology of the occupying forces. He is an icon for all journalists, wherever they are, to tell and write what is truth—not an ideology. He honored his chosen name Titus in the battle against corrupt teachings and violations of the truth.

Titus Brandsma is another one of those Catholics who changed the world we live in. He may not be widely known, but his example was courageous for the cause of freedom of the press for all nations and all ages.

12

Cafasso, Joseph: Prisons

Prisons are awful places to be in. I don't think anyone will deny that. No one wants to be there, yet we are willing to put some people in these places where we don't want to be ourselves. Nevertheless, somehow, prisons seem to be a necessary part of society. There have always been two different kinds of reasons why we say we need or want them. One reason, referred to as deterrence, claims that the primary purpose of prisons is to be so harsh and terrifying that they deter people from committing crimes out of fear of going to prison. The second reason, referred to as rehabilitation or moral reform, sees prisons as a place to better instruct prisoners in morality and proper behavior, and to prepare them for a better life.

No matter how we look at them, prisons are indeed not nice places to be in. Although the circumstances inside those places have gradually improved over the centuries, they are certainly not vacation resorts. Nevertheless, they are seen as places where we've "put away" some men and women with the idea, "They got what they deserved." It was in places like these that a special man brought some light in the darkness: Joseph Cafasso (1811-1860).

Joseph Cafasso was born in Italy of peasant parents. He studied at the seminary in Turin and was ordained in 1833. He continued his theological studies at the seminary and university of Turin and then at the Institute of St. Francis. Cafasso's body was twisted with curvature of the spine. Despite his deformed spine, Cafasso became a brilliant lecturer in moral theology there. Amazingly, in a society that looked down on the disabled, this shriveled little priest became a successful teacher, preacher and confessor. His life tells us to value people with physical deformities. And his example signifies hope to all disabled persons.

The prisons in Don Cafasso's time were gloomy places infested with pests. There was much communication among the prisoners because they did not have solitary cells, and the wicked had the greatest influence on all the others. It was among these outcasts of society that Don Cafasso spent most of his free time. He visited each prison at least once a week, and some of them once a day, and spent long hours there, usually four or five hours at a time. He also helped to get employment for those among the prisoners who were released from time to time. But most of all, he worked with prisoners to improve their terrible conditions.

His dedication to them was evident when this small and weak priest, with a curved spine, seized an enormous inmate by the beard and told him that he wouldn't let go until the man confessed his sins. Though he felt uncomfortable, the man began his confession, impelled by the priest's courage and ardor. Before long, the penitent was weeping; he emerged from the confessional giving praise to God. He told the other prisoners that he had never been so happy in his life and convinced them all to go to confession as well.

Don Cafasso singled out for special kindness criminals

condemned to death. He frequently visited all of them, instructed them, and prepared them for death. He accompanied them all the way to the scaffold—in total, fifty-seven from Turin prisons and seven others from other prisons. He helped many of them die at peace with God. He regarded these "hanged saints" as his favorite parishioners. No wonder, he became known as the "Priest of the Gallows."

In all of this, he was a follower of Jesus. Jesus has mercy for "the least," those despised by others. Convicts in particular rank high among "the least." For the general public, when a criminal gets prison time, the criminal is getting what is deserved; he needs to pay for what has been done. Nevertheless, Jesus condemns those about whom he says, "For I was… in prison and you did not care for me" (Mt. 25:42-43). Unfortunately, visiting prisoners is not so easy these days. Security measures have been strengthened and access is restricted. One needs to go through many discouraging procedures.

Yet, we can follow Don Cafasso's example and pray for those in prison, pray for their conversion as they deal with their troubled past. And, as they deal with separation from family and friends, we can pray that they will receive forgiveness—a second chance in life and continuing support. Instead of having an attitude of anger, retribution, punishment, or vengefulness, Jesus wants us to be merciful. Cafasso reminded us that we are all potential candidates for prison. Many of us are lucky to be a "step ahead of the law," because all of us have gotten away with something for which we deserve to be punished.

Joseph Cafasso is another one of those Catholics who changed the world we live in, especially the world of convicts and criminals, and the way we treat them.

13

Camillus de Lellis: Red Cross

When you need transportation to a hospital, you call an ambulance. When large disasters strike, we almost automatically rely on emergency help, especially from the Red Cross. When we need a blood transfusion, we may get blood from the Red Cross. We may not always be aware of it, but this hasn't always been that way. These things did not come out of the blue but had to be started somewhere by someone. That someone has largely remained unknown, but his name is Camillus de Lellis (1550-1640).

Camillus was born at Bocchianico, Italy. His father was a soldier, a mercenary who hired his services to whatever army would pay him the most. He spent little time at home and left the upbringing of Camillus to his mother.

Camillus was a rebellious youth, addicted to gambling. By age twenty-four he had literally lost his shirt to gambling. Attracted by the warrior model of his father, he fought for the Venetians against the Turks. Back in Naples, by 1574, he was penniless due to gambling. He decided to become a Capuchin novice, but was unable to be professed because of a diseased leg he had contracted while fighting the Turks. A running wound above his ankle would not heal. So Camillus went to the hospital

13 Camillus de Lellis: Red Cross

of San Giacomo in Rome, which took in hopeless cases. As he had no money to pay for a bed, he offered himself as a servant, asking in return that his persisting sore might be treated.

While working in that hospital, he noticed how the regular staff gave little attention to the patients, and he strived to do better. Camillus carefully selected five men from among his fellow-servants in the hospital. He told them of his ideal, and of the way he hoped to attain it. The men rose to his suggestion and agreed to throw in their lot with Camillus, pooling all their earnings, and living as much as possible together. Eventually he felt called to establish a religious community for this purpose.

Thus Camillus established the Order of Clerks Regular, Ministers of the Infirm (abbreviated as M.I.), better known as the Camillians. His experience in wars led him to establish a group of health care workers who would medically assist soldiers on the battlefield. Camillus received permission from Rome for them to have a large, red cross on their cassock. The large, red cross on their cassock has become a symbol of the Order. Camillians today continue to identify themselves with this emblem on their habits, a symbol universally recognized as the sign of charity and service. This was the original "Red Cross," hundreds of years before the secular International Red Cross organization was formed.

The next twenty years would see great expansion of the Congregation, with 15 houses of priests and brothers, and also 8 new hospitals. They championed some avant-garde medical practices, insisting, for example, on proper diet, fresh air and isolation of infected patients—long before this became general practice in hospitals. His men would also offer their assistance to troops fighting in Hungary and Croatia in 1595, forming the first recorded military field ambulance.

Soon Camillus realized that the sick outside hospitals were in far more need of good nursing than those within. So when pestilence broke out, Camillus oversaw the Congregation's involvement in helping the sick in the harbor of Naples. He and his men went to the plague victims on the quarantined galleys, prohibited from entering the city. Members of the Order devoted themselves to these victims of the Bubonic plague. But several of his Camillians also died themselves from helping the sick, thus becoming the first martyrs of charity. It was due to these efforts that the people of Rome credited Camillus with ridding the city of a great plague and the subsequent famine. Soon, he became known as the "Saint of Rome."

Camillus not only took care of the proper treatment of the sick, but he also extended his concern to the end of their lives. He had come to be aware of the many cases of people being buried alive, due to haste, and so he ordered that the Brothers of his Order wait fifteen minutes past the moment when patients seemed to have drawn their last breath, in order to avoid their premature burial. All of this happened as early as the sixteenth century.

Camillus is another one of those Catholics who changed the world we live in. We are indebted to him for the institution of the Red Cross and for the introduction of military field ambulances—the beginning of what has become now standard practice.

14

Canisius, Peter: The Catechism

If you have a message that is important for people around you, you need some kind of communication tool. People still living in forested areas, for instance, use smoke signals and drums for long-distance communication, but those tools are quite primitive. Not too long ago, papyrus, parchment and paper became the main tools of communication. Once the printing press had been invented (§34), messages could spread even more easily and quickly. The first ones who realized this were the Protestant Reformers in Germany during the 16th century.

Though the printing press was developed in the late 1400s, Catholics had not made much use of it until Peter Canisius (1521-1597) came along. While the Protestants were busy developing their Protestant catechisms in the vernacular, Peter responded with his own catechism, thereby marking the beginning of the Catholic press. Canisius had a message for the world! He believed that to defend Catholic truths with the pen was just as important as to convert Hindus. People listened to him because he wrote and spoke without the bitterness and ridicule that was so common among other writers on both sides of the Reformation slit in those days. Who was this Peter?

The Dutchman Pieter de Houndt—better known by the Latin version of his name, Peter Canisius—was born in Nijmegen, in what is now called the Netherlands. He was born shortly after Luther had begun his open rebellion against the Catholic Church in Germany. During his study at the University of Cologne, Canisius met Peter Faber, one of the first companions of Ignatius of Loyola (§38). Through him, Canisius became the first Dutchman to join the newly founded Society of Jesus in 1543.

Canisius lived his adult life at a time when the Catholic Church had to confront the *Protestant* Reformation with what is often called the Counter-Reformation, but which should more properly be called the *Catholic* Reformation. Canisius had a message for the world, but he realized that the German language had been the most powerful stronghold of the Protestant Reformation. Protestants were given German sermons, read the Bible in German, sang German hymns and soon lost through this alone their union with Rome. The traditional connection of Germany with the Latin culture of the Roman Church had thus been lost. So he knew his own important message, too, had to be in German.

Besides, it had to be written in the right tone, defensive rather than offensive. He was very definite on that. He rejected hostile attacks against the Reformers: "With words like these, we don't cure patients, we make them incurable." As he put it, "An honest explanation of the faith would be much more effective than a polemical attack against reformers." He was of the opinion that "people should be attracted and won to the simplicity of the faith as much by example as by argument." Therefore, "they should be led gently and gradually to those dogmas about which there is dispute."

That was the beginning of his next, most important move.

14 Canisius, Peter: The Catechism

For many years, Peter had witnessed how the students in his universities were swayed by the flashy speeches and the well-written arguments of the Protestants, who had begun producing catechisms and bibles in the vernacular soon after the invention of the printing press. Catholics, on the other hand, had been slow to take advantage of the new technology. Canisius, however, saw the need for a Catholic catechism that would present true Catholic beliefs undistorted by fanatics. Obviously, the printing press could create an effective way of communication. The Catholic press was the vital tool for his message to Catholics. The train was set into motion.

By the end of 1554, Canisius' catechism was at the press and was published in March 1555 with the title *Summary of Christian Doctrine*. It was intended for college students and, thus, it was in Latin. Canisius then translated it into German in 1556 and worked on an adaptation for secondary school students, which he called *Shorter Catechism*. It was well-organized and so easy to understand that a special version was printed for younger children, which he called *Catholic Catechism*.

The Catechism became one of the most successful religious bestsellers in Church history. It met the need of the day and was intended to counter the divisive effect of Luther's Catechism. During Peter's lifetime, this *Catechism* had at least 200 editions, was translated into fifteen languages, and had to be reprinted more than two hundred times. Besides, it was the most frequently issued publication by a Dutch author ever: 1,075 different editions in 26 different languages until the 20th century. Catholics in Germany were even calling the *Catechism* simply "*the Canisius.*" His catechism generated the Catholic Reformation as Luther's catechism had spread the Protestant Reformation.

Peter's Catechism was a communication tool that was much more defensive than offensive. He wanted to explain and defend the Catholic faith as it had been formulated at the Council of Trent. He had attended several sessions of the Council of Trent himself, accompanying the Bishop of Augsburg as a theological adviser. So he was well suited to define the basic principles of Catholicism in the German language and make them more accessible to readers in German-speaking countries. That was his message which he saw fit to be spread through the printing press. And it became an powerful tool of mass communication.

For a half-century, Peter Canisius would lead the Catholic Reformation in the German speaking countries of Austria, Bavaria, and Bohemia. He never slowed down until his death. When someone asked him how he coped with this work load, Peter replied, "If you have too much to do, with God's help you will find time to do it all." With astounding energy, he preached and taught in parishes, reformed and founded universities, wrote many books including popular catechisms, restored lapsed Catholics, converted Protestants, preached retreats, and still found time to care for the sick.

In his last thirty years traveling more than twenty thousand miles on foot or horseback, Peter spearheaded the renewal of the Catholic faith in German areas. In 1591, at the age of 70, Canisius suffered a stroke which left him partially paralyzed, but he continued to preach and write with the aid of a secretary until his death in Fribourg. In the meantime, he had reclaimed whole provinces from Protestantism, founded several Jesuit colleges, and left behind him 1110 Jesuits when he died.

He left a rich legacy behind. Canisius really was the *Catechist* of Germany for centuries, and formed people's Catholic faith for centuries. He played such a key role in

14 Canisius, Peter: The Catechism

Germany that he has often been called the "second apostle of Germany," in reference to what Boniface had done for Germany centuries ago. His mission was not only to Germany, but also to the rest of Europe, and soon to the rest of the world. All Catholic countries would soon have some kind of catechism, either as a translation of Canisius' catechism or written on its pattern.

When we talk about "the catechism" today, we are most likely referring to the *Catechism of the Catholic Church*, promulgated by Pope John Paul II in 1992 to coincide with the 30th anniversary of the opening of the Second Vatican Council. For more than a decade, bishops, theologians and other experts had worked on a compendium of all Catholic doctrine regarding both faith and morals, similar to what Canisius had done all by himself. The fruit of their work was an organized presentation of the essential teachings of the Catholic Church in the light of the Second Vatican Council and the whole of the Church's tradition. It sums up, in book form, the beliefs of the Catholic faithful.

The 1992 catechism was new, but the idea behind it certainly was not. In 1566, the so-called Roman Catechism—the catechism of Canisius—was published three years after the Council of Trent. Similar to the 1566 catechism of Canisius more than three centuries before, the 1992 Catechism became an international best-seller. Right after being elected as Pope, John Paul II told the cardinals who elected him that he saw that his main work was to implement the teachings of the Second Vatican Council, which is similar to what Canisius wanted to do with the teachings of the Council of Trent. When we read the new catechism, we should keep in mind that Canisius had prepared and shown the way. Both catechisms had and still have a message in print for the world at large.

Canisius is another one of those Catholics who changed the

world we live in. He gave the world a Catholic Catechism!

15

Carrel, Alexis: Miracles

These days, the power of medical technology is greater than ever before. The latest medical achievements are so incredible that people often speak of "miracles" performed by medical doctors. Of course, they are not really miracles, for they can all be explained by *natural* causes.

When people speak of real miracles, they usually mean that only *supernatural* causes can explain them. Are such miracles really possible? Many think nowadays they are not, for they believe in naturalism—the idea or belief that only natural (as opposed to supernatural) laws and forces operate in this world. They believe there are no such things as supernatural causes. It is an age-old discussion that came to a head with Alexis Carrel (1873-1944).

Alexis Carrel came from a devout Catholic family and was educated by the Jesuits. By the time he entered the University, he no longer practiced his religion, but had become a strong believer in science and medicine—fed by a strong belief in naturalism. Based on his tremendous achievements in his field, he was awarded the Nobel Prize in Physiology or Medicine in 1912 for pioneering vascular suturing techniques. He invented the first perfusion pump with Charles A. Lindbergh, thereby eventually opening the way to organ transplantation.

Amazingly enough, this stanch defender of naturalism would gradually free himself from the shackles of naturalism and open himself to the world of supernatural causes. But it was a very tedious and long process. What made the final outcome very convincing is that he, who had been an expert in the world of natural causes, learned there was also a world of supernatural causes. G. K. Chesterton once said, "Take away the supernatural, and what remains is the unnatural."

This slow process of conversion was set into motion when Carrel witnessed, at close range, a miraculous cure in Lourdes. A fellow doctor, a former classmate of his, had asked Carrel to take his place as the doctor in charge of a train carrying sick people to Lourdes. Carrel was interested in Lourdes, but not because he wanted to check on the authenticity of miracles. At that time and for many years afterwards, he did not believe in miracles. He merely wanted to see with his own eyes the fast rate of the healing of wounds reported from Lourdes. Yet, Carrel very much hoped that nobody in the medical community would learn about his trip to Lourdes. He knew that the mere rumor of it would jeopardize his career in the Medical Faculty of the University of Lyons, where at that time he was assistant professor of anatomy.

It was in Lourdes that Carrel witnessed two miraculous cures. The first one was in 1902. The second one took place in 1910, when he saw the sudden restoration of the sight of an 18-month-old boy who was born blind. By far the more famous of the two cures is the first one, though. It took place on May 28, 1902. It is known as "the Marie Bailly case." Indeed it is so famous that it is not possible to write on Carrel without discussing it, however briefly.

Marie Bailly was born in 1878. Both her father, an optician, and her mother died of tuberculosis. Of her five siblings only one was free of that disease. She was twenty when she first showed symptoms of pulmonary tuberculosis. A year later she was diagnosed with tuberculous meningitis, from which she suddenly recovered when she used Lourdes water. In two more years, in 1901, she came down with tubercular peritonitis. Soon she could not retain food. In March 1902 doctors in Lyons refused to operate on her for fear that she would die on the operating table. On May 25, 1902, she begged her friends to smuggle her onto a train that carried sick people to Lourdes. She had to be smuggled because, as a rule, such trains were forbidden to carry dying people.

In Lourdes, Marie Bailly was examined by several doctors. On May 27, she insisted on being carried to the Grotto, although the doctors were afraid that she would die on her way there. Carrel himself took such a grim view of her condition that he vowed to become a monk if she reached the Grotto alive, a mere quarter of a mile from the hospital.

Meanwhile Carrel followed her and stood behind her, with a notepad in his hands. He marked the time, the pulse, the facial expression, and other clinical details as he witnessed under his very eyes the following: the enormously distended and very hard abdomen began to flatten, and within thirty minutes it had completely disappeared. No discharge whatsoever was observed from the body.

Carrel continued to take a great interest in her. He asked a psychiatrist to test her every two weeks, which was done for four months. She was regularly tested for traces of tuberculosis. In late November, she was declared to be in good health both physically and mentally. In December she entered the novitiate in Paris. Without ever having a relapse, she lived the arduous life of a Sister of Charity until 1937, when she died 35 years later, at the age of 58.

Carrel was one of those who had personally witnessed a real miracle and yet, for a long time, still did not believe. He kept claiming that medical science must keep its eyes open to unusual cures, even if they took place at Lourdes or other pilgrimage places. He was still a strong believer in naturalism—a faith as strong as, if not stronger than, a religious faith. As Doctor Olivieri, president of the Lourdes Medical Bureau from 1959 to 1971, put it, "So, when one tells these people about miraculous cures, they always have a ready response—they are due to as yet undiscovered causes, or to all sorts of natural causes… or will be able to be explained later… In the end, what all these explanations have in common is the a priori fundamental principle that 'miracles don't exist.' To which I reply: 'Miracles do exist.'" Indeed, we must not forget that a miraculous cure is much more than a purely medical matter, however interesting.

Gradually, very slowly, Carrel was beginning to see an opening for the supernatural. He no longer refused to discount a supernatural explanation, even writing a book describing his experience (though it was not published until four years after his death). He took to task the members of the medical community who refused to look at facts whenever they appeared to be miraculous. However, it was to be expected that this stance was a detriment to his career and reputation among his fellow doctors—so much so that he had the feeling there was no future in academic medicine in France. He decided to migrate to Canada with the intention of farming and raising cattle. After a brief period, he accepted an appointment at the University of Chicago and two years later at the Rockefeller Institute of Medical Research.

Now that Alexis Carrel, a medical authority with the credentials of a Nobel Laureate, had accepted the miracle of Marie Bailly, one would think the Catholic Church should be ready to accept Marie's miracle as well. But the Church wasn't! The Catholic Church certainly believes in miracles, but not without thorough investigation, done by the *International Medical Committee of Lourdes* (C.M.I.L.). This Committee has been in existence since 1947 and is made up of some 20 members, respected in their own particular medical field. A two-third majority is required for an affirmative vote. The medical result is sent to the bishop of the diocese where the cured person lives. The bishop can then decide or abstain from recognizing the "miraculous" character of that particular cure.

The Committee is extremely cautious in its decisions. Because it is logically impossible to say that something is "inexplicable," they can only say that it is "unexplained." The International Committee decided against recommending Marie Bailly's cure for ecclesiastical approval because earlier doctors had not even thought of the possibility of a false pregnancy (*pseudosciosis*). As the physicist Fr. Stanley Jaki remarks, one's first reaction to this may be that it is self-defeating to be so careful in excluding the possibility of an error.

Yet, this is the kind of caution which the Church has always demanded from doctors as they are consulted in evaluating cures that appear miraculous. It is better to err to the side of caution than to jump to false conclusions. Even the Sisters of Charity had subjected Marie Bailly's health to close scrutiny. Only when they were fully satisfied did they accept her as a postulant, so that she could depart in late November, 1892, from Lyons, to begin her novitiate in Paris.

The caution on the side of the Committee remained. But this didn't change the fact that Alexis Carrel had become convinced that he had witnessed a miracle. Carrel died as a genuinely devout Catholic. His Catholic death is all the more significant because for most of his life, Carrel was a resolute agnostic. Indeed it took a special resolve, and another special miracle, to give up his agnosticism. He finally could say, "In man, the things which are not measurable are more important than those which are measurable."

Alexis Carrel is another one of those Catholics who changed the world we live in. He showed the world that there are miracles beyond medical explanation.

16

Catherine of Siena: Feminism

When people hear the term "feminism," they usually associate it with a whole series of other ideas: pro-choice, reproductive rights, trans-women, sexual freedom and so many others. That's rather unfortunate, for these associations have probably tainted the term "feminism" in the minds of many. Instead, it should be stated that this form of feminism should actually be called "radical feminism," to distinguish it from a more moderate, Christian version of feminism. Radical feminists share a rather visceral hostility towards the Church's position on issues such as abortion and marriage—and more in general, they think women must reclaim their sexuality from being dominated by a hierarchy of celibate men who presumably cannot understand women's issues. In general, one could say their opinions are more anti-Church than pro-women.

The radical feminist paradigm still focuses on a vision of sexual equality that prizes autonomy above all—the autonomy of "self-determination," even in matters of the life and death of others, even of the unborn. It is this radical form of feminism that the Church rejects. Pope Benedict XVI once said, "[W]hat feminism promotes in its radical form is no longer the

Christianity that we know; it is another religion." The Church's stand against abortion, for instance, is to protect human life, not to demean women. In other words, being against radical feminists is not the same as being against women.

As a matter of fact, there is also a Christian version of feminism. Pope John Paul II, for example, aligned himself with women's quest for freedom and adopted much of the language of the women's movement, even calling for a "new feminism" in his Encyclical *Evangelium Vitae*. A person who perfectly fits in this feminist mode is Catherine of Siena (1347-1380).

Catherine of Siena was a Dominican tertiary and mystic of considerable influence who was proclaimed a Doctor of the Church in 1970. Considered by her contemporaries as having high levels of spiritual insight, she participated in the highest levels of public life through corresponding with the princes of Italy, consulting with papal legates, and acting as a diplomat negotiating among the city states of Italy. She counseled for reform of the clergy and was influential in convincing Pope Gregory XI to leave Avignon—a papal residency for nearly 70 years—and restore the Holy See to Rome.

It is not so difficult to understand why some feminists wish to claim her patronage. A short version of her life goes like this: At seven years of age she determined she wasn't the marrying type. When pressured by her parents to submit to an arranged marriage, at age twelve, she defiantly cut off her hair and fasted to rebel against her parents' wishes. Surprisingly, she did not join a convent, but instead became actively involved in political circles unknown to women. She arbitrated family feuds. She brokered peace within and between the city-states of Tuscany. Bankers, generals, princes, dukes, kings and queens, as well as scholars and abbots sought her counsel. Catherine's greatest political success was also a spiritual triumph—convincing Pope

Gregory XI to return the papacy from France to Rome. Christopher Check, President of *Catholic Answers*, summarizes her life this way: "A real glass-ceiling breaker, Catherine made it big in a man's world."

Listen to what this *woman* wrote to the highest *man* in the Church hierarchy, Pope Gregory XI: "Most Holy Father,... because [Christ] has given you authority and because you have accepted it, you ought to use your virtue and power. If you do not wish to use it, it might be better for you to resign what you have accepted; it would give more honor to God and health to your soul.... If you do not do this, you will be censured by God. If I were you, I would fear that Divine Judgment might descend on me."

Well, here is the kicker. In marked contrast to radical feminism, Catherine never understood herself as a pioneer for women's rights, much less a model for narcissistic self-fulfillment. On the contrary, she put into practice the truth her Holy Bridegroom had revealed to her: "I am that which is; you are that which is not." As Christopher Check remarks, "Because she commanded the actions of the pope, it is doubtless this action which most excites the feminists. Alas, they entirely miss the point. At no time ever in her correspondence with Pope Gregory, which is indeed direct, does she question his authority. On the contrary she tells him, '"Esto vir!' Be a man! Use your authority."

Catherine of Siena is another one of those Catholics who changed the world we live in. She showed the world how women can and must use their feminine talents and powers for the good of all.

17

Chesterton, G. K.: Common Sense

We live in a world that has taught itself to doubt almost everything with questions such as: Is there anything? Can we believe anything? Is there truth? Is there a God? The confusing philosophies of our time that raise such questions are relativism, agnosticism, skepticism, secularism, nihilism and the like. They basically come from people who "specialize" in questioning everything on earth by calling themselves philosophers. There is this joke among scientists that uses warnings like "Don't touch anything in a physics lab," or "Don't taste anything in a chemistry lab," or "Don't smell anything in a biology lab." But perhaps we should add to the list, "Don't buy anything in a philosophy department."

Is there anything that can bring us back to truth and reality? The answer comes from G. K. Chesterton (1874-1936). His answer is: yes, *common sense*! No wonder, in the title of Dale Ahlquist's book, he is called "The Apostle of Common Sense." Who is this man?

Gilbert Keith (G. K.) Chesterton was born in London and baptized in the Church of England. Ironically, he didn't learn to read until he was 8 years old, but he would eventually be a prolific and scholarly author of 17 nonfiction books, 9 fiction

17 Chesterton, G. K.: Common Sense

books and numerous essays and poems. Chesterton married Frances Blogg in 1901; the marriage lasted the rest of his life. Chesterton credited Frances with leading him back to Anglicanism, though he later considered Anglicanism to be a "pale imitation" of the true Church. He entered into full communion with the Catholic Church in 1922. Surprisingly, he wrote many of his famous Father Brown mysteries—with this quiet, unassuming priest who solves mysteries like Sherlock Holmes—before joining the Roman Catholic Church in 1922.

What does common sense mean in Chesterton's writings? He himself wrote, "The surprising thing about common sense is how uncommon it has become. And common things are the basis of common sense even though common things are not commonplace." In other words, common sense is no longer common—what is common is not sense, but nonsense. Therefore, using "uncommon sense" is saying things that are nonsensical.

What does this actually mean? Common sense appeals to realities that we all know to be real and true even if we cannot prove them. Common sense is about what we all have in common. The ultimate thing we have in common is our Creator. Thus, common sense is a religious truth. Harriet Beecher Stowe defined common sense another way: "Common sense is seeing things as they are; and doing things as they should be." Chesterton used slightly different words when he asserted "that truth exists whether we like it or not, and that it is for us to accommodate ourselves to it."

Let's apply common sense, for instance, to a question like "Is there anything?" We should begin by answering "Yes." If, instead, we had begun by answering "No," it would not be the beginning, but the end of the question. As Fr. James Schall puts it, "I myself have all the levels of being in my very existence. I weigh, grow, feel and think. I am the one being in the universe with a hand connected to a mind. Thus, I can understand things.... My thoughts reach the world through my hand." Thus reality is within our reach.

Something similar can be said against skepticism. Chesterton put it this way, "Most fundamental sceptics appear to survive because they are not consistently skeptical and not at all fundamental. They will first deny everything and then admit something, if for the sake of argument or often rather of attack without argument." More in general, "What a man can believe depends upon his philosophy, not upon the clock or the century"—not on the various philosophies that pop up now and then, here and there. Instead, we need a "sound" philosophy of common sense.

Chesterton wrote about everything—politics, science, technology, philosophy, psychology, morality, history and even economics. Basically, Chesterton had the unique ability to interweave paradox, wit and common sense while writing about topics that helped the reader better understand God, themselves, society and the world they live in. He saw the forest where everyone else saw only trees.

Yet, he was just a man. He drank. He smoked. At 300 pounds, he enjoyed his meals more than most. In short, he was real—real enough that now, eighty years after the beloved English writer and author's death, a British bishop has opened an investigation into whether Chesterton can, in fact, be declared a Saint. Time will tell.

Chesterton is another one of those Catholics who changed the world we live in. He gave the world its common sense back.

18

Claver, Peter: Slave Trade

If you would ask citizens in our society whether slave trade is right or wrong, almost everyone would say it's wrong. But, as we all know, that hasn't always been the case; slave trade was once accepted by large majorities of peoples. Why, then, would slave trade be wrong? Human beings differ in so many respects, perhaps some beings could very well be inferior to others and could therefore be traded like cattle? Why not?

The latter reasoning is obviously flawed. But how do we know this? The legendary American President Abraham Lincoln of all people showed the fallacy of using comparisons and relative criteria when judging the value of human beings. He applied this argument also to the contentious moral issue of slavery. His point was that all the answers slave holders and slave traders might come up with to defend their "moral claims" use *relative* criteria—for instance, it is considered morally right to enslave people with a darker skin color or with a lower intelligence. If you think so, someone with an even lighter skin or higher intelligence might show up and claim the "moral right" to enslave you, too, because those criteria are entirely relative. As Lincoln said, "By this rule, you are to be slave to the first man you meet, with a fairer skin than your own.... By this rule, you are to be slave to the first man you meet, with an intellect superior to your own." This is a serious warning for those who decide what is right or wrong by using comparisons and relative criteria. We need another rule to prove that trading slaves and owning slaves is right.

So why is slave trade wrong then? The person who showed the world that there is only one reason why slave trade is wrong was Peter Claver (1581–1654), a Spanish Jesuit priest.

Peter Claver was born to a prosperous family in Verdu, Spain, and joined the Jesuits in 1601. When he was in Majorca studying philosophy, Claver was encouraged by Alphonsus Rodriguez, the saintly Jesuit Brother and doorkeeper of the college, to go to the missions in America. Claver listened, and in 1610, he landed in Cartagena, Colombia, the center of the slave trade.

Cartagena was a slave-trading hub. 10,000 slaves poured into the port yearly, after crossing the Atlantic from West Africa under conditions so foul that an estimated one-third died in transit. By this time, the slave trade had been established in the Americas for about a century. Since local natives were considered not physically suited to work in the gold and silver mines, this created a demand for blacks from Angola and Congo. These were bought into West Africa for four crowns a head, or bartered for goods and sold in America for an average two hundred crowns apiece. Others were captured at random, especially able-bodied males and females deemed suitable for hard labor.

Between the years 1616 and 1650, Peter Claver worked daily to minister to the needs of some 10,000 slaves who arrived each year. When a ship came in, Peter first begged for food to bring to the slaves—bread, dates, medicines, brandy, tobacco and cologne. He then went on board with translators to bring his gifts as well as his skills as a doctor and teacher. As he used to say, "we must speak to them with our hands before we try to speak to them with our lips."

Claver also managed to convince the local authorities to issue a law that no new arrivals be baptized until they received adequate instruction. He then used this law to delay their departure into a life of slavery by prolonging his catechism classes, much to the chagrin of the slave traders. Peter Claver baptized more than 300,000 slaves by 1651, when he himself became a victim of the plague.

What was Claver's reason, or motive, for doing all of this for slaves? Why did he *not* consider them inferior to other human beings? The only reason is his deep belief that we are all God's children, whether white or black, rich or poor. We are all part of the same human race, sharing the same human dignity, so all other people are our brothers and sisters.

It was this very belief that incited him to labor unceasingly for the salvation of the African slaves and the abolition of the Black slave trade. He is considered a heroic example of what should be the Christian praxis of love and of the exercise of human rights (§46). No wonder, the Congress of the Republic of Colombia declared September 9 as the national Human Rights Day in his honor.

Peter Claver is another one of those Catholics who changed the world we live in. He showed us by his faith and by example the evil of the slave trade. He had vowed to be "the slave of the enslaved Africans forever."

19

Constantine the Great: A Breakthrough

The world has some 2.3 billion Christians at the present time—31.2% of the entire world population. That is hard to believe when you think of the meager beginnings of Christianity after the crucifixion of Jesus Christ. How could Christianity expand so much and so rapidly? Part of the explanation is the enormous work of the Apostle Paul in countries around the Mediterranean (§52). But probably a more influential role was played by Roman Emperor Constantine the Great (272-337).

When the emperor of the West, Constantius, died in Britain in 306, the army hailed his son Constantine as the new emperor. There was Christian influence in his family somewhere, for Constantine had a half-sister named Anastasia, which means "Resurrection."

When Constantine's co-emperor in the East, Maxentius, declared war to Constantine, after building an army in Italy of over 100,000 troops, Constantine decided, although he had fewer than 40,000 troops, not to wait but attack him on his own territory. After a chain of victories, Constantine found himself across the Tiber from Rome. That's when he had a vision of God showing him a symbol—an X [*Chi*] with a P [*Rho*] superimposed on it, known to Christians as the first two Greek

19 Constantine the Great: A Breakthrough

(capital) letters of the word *Christ*—and telling him to make this his standard. Constantine emblazoned this Christian emblem on banners and on the shields of his soldiers.

It was Constantine's hope that Christianity would help him unify his empire—and in fact it did—but soon he would realize the roles would need to be reversed too: the empire would need to help unify Christianity because there was a new rift lurking at the horizon of the Church, and therefore indirectly of the empire. Its name was Arianism (§5). One of its strongest selling points was that it could get "Christianity" more easily accepted by a wide variety of otherwise hesitant Roman citizens, most of them pagans.

The man behind Arianism, Arius, had fled to Nicomedia where Emperor Constantine had his imperial palace. When Constantine heard of the new heresy, he initially wondered what all the commotion was about, but he was soon informed more accurately by a bishop friend. So he summoned a large assembly of bishops to resolve the matter in the nearby city of Nicaea. Never before had a Council of bishops been convened by a Roman emperor. Never before had the government paid for the travelling costs of the attendees. What had never been done before by a Council either was that the attending bishops—between 250 and 300—expressed Church teaching by drafting a Creed that we still recite in most of our churches.

At the end, Emperor Constantine wrote to all the churches of the empire, "the judgment of three hundred bishops cannot be other than the judgment of God." Arius and two diehards were exiled. It was this Council of Nicaea that would protect Christianity from a dangerous heresy—indirectly thanks to the efforts of Constantine.

On the other hand, there are many myths surrounding the life of Constantine. Never did he make Christianity the official religion of the empire—Theodosius would, forty years later. Never did he himself become Christian, until just before his death, when he was baptized by an Arian bishop. Neither was he the first emperor to legalize Christianity—that was Gallerius. All he did was using Christianity as a model for unity and stability in his empire. Yet, he was very "generous" to the Church, even to the point of being "dedicated" to the Church. All in all, he played a vital role in the rapid expansion of Christianity.

So our question is now: was Constantine a real Catholic-Christian emperor? Perhaps not in the strict sense, but at least he was very sympathetic to the Church. He did mint coins that contained the Chi-Rho symbol. He did promulgate, together with the new emperor of the Eastern half, Licinius, a worldwide decree, known as the Edict of Milan (313), which allowed all citizens of the entire empire to follow their religious beliefs in peace. This edict changed Christianity from a persecuted to an officially favored religion. Also did Constantine give a large property from the Lateran family to the Church for the construction of a basilica and residence of the pope—called to this very day St. John Lateran. In addition, he did erect a basilica over the tomb of St. Peter on the hill across the Tiber known as the Vatican.

Constantine is another one of those Catholics who changed the world we live in. He Christianized the world and by doing so had an enormous impact on all of history.

20

Copernicus, Nicolaus: Heliocentrism

The popular view nowadays is that it was Galileo who "discovered" that the earth revolves around the sun. Actually, the notion of a revolving earth is at least as old as the ancient Greeks. In the 3rd century BC, Aristarchus of Samos had already played with a heliocentric model. But the geocentric theory—with the earth in the center—endorsed by Aristotle and given mathematical plausibility by Ptolemy, remained the prevailing model for many centuries.

However, the Aristotelian-Ptolemaic theory was such a complex system, with its numerous epicycles—circles moving on other circles—that hardly anyone believed that it corresponded to the physical reality of the Universe. It accounted for observations and could be used in predicting the position of heavenly bodies and it could help ships navigate the seas, so it was basically nothing more than a rather effective mathematical model—in other words, it just "saved the appearances," to use the words of Thomas Aquinas. According to this view, any astronomical theory, or any physical theory for that matter, was nothing more than a convenient ordering of data with not necessarily an intrinsic bearing on reality.

This view of the world and the universe did not change much until Nicolaus Copernicus (1473-1543) came along. Copernicus was a convincing astronomer who replaced the Aristotelian-Ptolemaic theory with the idea that the Earth was not the center of the Universe but that it (along with other celestial bodies) rather revolved around the Sun.

Copernicus was a Polish astronomer—probably not a priest as often claimed, but a Canon and a Third Order or Secular Dominican. In 1543, he published *On the Revolution of the Heavenly Spheres*, in which he supported heliocentricity: the Sun is in the center with the Earth moving around it. Copernicus, a good and faithful Catholic, published his book at the urging of two eminent prelates, and dedicated it to Pope Paul III, who received it cordially. The publisher of Copernicus' book, which was published just before his death in 1543, had asked Andreas Osiander, a Lutheran clergyman, to write a preface to the book because he knew that it would be attacked by Protestants—which it was—for its opposition to Scripture. Osiander also knew that the Protestant Reformers Luther and Melanchthon violently opposed any suggestions that the earth revolved around the sun. So he wrote an unsigned preface, which everyone took to be from Copernicus himself, presenting the heliocentrism theory as a mere *hypothesis* (not a proven fact) for charting the movements of the planets in a simpler manner than the burdensome Ptolemaic system. The Catholic Church gave no censure to Copernicus, and the book was well-received by Jesuit astronomers of the time.

Did Copernicus prove that the earth circles the sun? No, his theory was indeed no more than a very plausible *hypothesis*. Besides, the Copernican model with its circular orbits—instead of the upcoming more accurate elliptical orbits of Johannes

Kepler (1571-1630)—would still need the so despised epicycles of the Ptolemaic model to correct for its own inaccuracy. In other words, there was no conclusive evidence for Copernicus' heliocentrism—it was a hypothesis in need of further proof.

In addition, there was a rather serious problem for heliocentrism. Aristotle himself had pointed this out already nearly two thousand years earlier. If the Earth did orbit the Sun, the philosopher wrote, then stellar parallaxes would be observable in the sky. In other words, there would be a shift in position of a star observed from the earth on one side of the sun, and then six months later from the other side. True, given the still simple technology of Copernicus' time, no such shifts in their positions could possibly be observed, given the stars' great distance, as it would require more sensitive measuring equipment than was available at the time to document the existence of these shifts. The case was in fact not decided until 1838, when Friedrich Bessel succeeded in determining the parallax of star 61 Cygni.

When Galileo Galilei, almost a century later, was eager to adopt and promote heliocentrism, the lack of proof was still a problem, although Galileo tried to hide or even ignore the problem. Yet, the heliocentric model with the Sun at the center of our Universe held more or less fast until the 1920s when it was first shown that the Sun wasn't the center of the Universe either.

Nicolaus Copernicus is another one of those Catholics who changed the world we live in—not the way the world is, of course, but the way we look at the world.

21

Cyril and Methodius: The Vernacular

Catholics who attend a Mass in Germany, for instance, can expect a liturgy in German and readings in German. Were it a Mass in France, the liturgy would be in French and the readings in French. That hasn't always been that way. Originally Masses were said either in Greek (in the eastern half of the Roman Empire) or in Latin (in the western half of the empire). That split had not always been there either. For a long time, the common language and culture of the entire Mediterranean world was Greek. Most Christians were used to the Greek language in their Bible translations. Greek was even the language prevailing in Christian Rome until around the year 200.

But when the Romans expanded their empire, the situation changed: Latin was mostly used in the government and the army, while Greek was used in schools and the marketplace. No wonder the inscription of Jesus' cross was written in three languages: in Aramaic, the local language of Jesus, and in Latin and Greek, the two common languages of the empire.

However, culture was slowly changing all across the Roman Empire, most notably in its western part, and so was the knowledge of Greek. Tertullian in Carthage, in present-day

21 Cyril and Methodius: The Vernacular

Tunisia, would become the first Christian Church Father to write in Latin. Soon Jerome would start his translation of the Bible into Latin (§35). Latin had actually become "the language of the people." His Bible translation is therefore called the *Vulgate*, the "people's version."

Latin remained the universal language of Europe for centuries after. Scholars and scientists published everything in Latin so that more people could read it. The first scientist to publish extensively in his native language was Galileo, who wrote in Italian and was then translated to Latin so that more people might read his work. And the Catholic Church was no exception. Mass was said in Latin until the Second Vatican Council in the 1960s. Nevertheless, Latin was gradually losing its status as "the language of the people." The people preferred more and more their own local language, which is called the *vernacular*—the language or dialect spoken by the ordinary people in a particular country or region. A milestone in this process was reached when Cyril and Methodius appeared on the scene.

Cyril and Methodius were two brothers, born in Thessalonica, in present-day Greece—Cyril in about 827-828 and Methodius about 815-820. It is not clear whether Cyril and Methodius were of Slavic or Byzantine Greek origin, or both. After their ordination, they were sent by the pope as missionaries to Moravia (now part of the Czech Republic). For the purpose of this mission, they devised a new alphabet, that would become the Cyrillic alphabet, which is still used by many languages today. The newly made priests officiated in their own languages at the altars of some of the principal churches. Cyril and Methodius were dedicated to the ideal of expressing faith and liturgy in a people's native language—in the vernacular, that is.

They composed a Slavonic liturgy, highly uncommon then. That and their free use of the vernacular in preaching led to opposition from the German clergy. The German bishop refused to consecrate Slavic priests, and Cyril was forced to appeal to Rome. On their visit to Rome, the two brothers had the joy of seeing their new liturgy approved by Pope Adrian II, who formally authorized the use of the new Slavic liturgy—certainly a new development over the monopoly of Latin and Greek in the Catholic Church.

Through their work they influenced the cultural development of all Slavs, for which they received the title "Apostles to the Slavs." Cyrillic eventually spread throughout most of the Slavic world to become the standard alphabet in the Eastern Orthodox Slavic countries. Hence, Cyril and Methodius' efforts also paved the way for the spread of Christianity throughout Eastern Europe.

The two brothers are now Patrons of Moravia, specially venerated by Catholic Czechs, Slovaks, Croatians, Orthodox Serbians and Bulgarians. In 1980, Pope John Paul II named them additional co-patrons of Europe. Their legacy can still be found in the Eastern Catholic Churches or Oriental Catholic Churches, also called the Eastern-rite Catholic Churches and Greek Catholic Churches. All in all, there are twenty-three Eastern Christian particular churches in full communion with the Pope in Rome, as part of the worldwide Catholic Church.

Cyril and Methodius are two of those Catholics who changed the world we live in. They were the first to break the barriers of Greek and Latin in the Catholic Church to open the church doors for the vernacular.

22

Damien de Veuster: Leprosy

Although leprosy is not a disease that all countries have to deal with, it is a serious problem for most countries in tropical areas all over the world. The disease is caused by a bacterium that resembles the bacterium causing tuberculosis. Initially, infections are without symptoms and typically remain this way for 5 to 20 years.

For a long time, the disease was considered very contagious, which made lepers outcasts. The Bible testifies to this ordeal: "The garments of one afflicted with a scaly infection shall be rent and the hair disheveled, and the mustache covered. The individual shall cry out, 'Unclean, unclean!' As long as the infection is present, the person shall be unclean. Being unclean, that individual shall dwell apart, taking up residence outside the camp." (Lev. 13:45-46).

Only recently it was discovered that the disease is not highly contagious. But most harm had already been done. It can now be cured with a multidrug therapy. These treatments are provided free of charge by the World Health Organization. So times have changed considerably. But that has not always been the case. For centuries, lepers were avoided like the "pest," and forced to cry out "Unclean! Unclean!" To fight this awful destiny, a special person was needed: The Belgian priest Damien de Veuster (1840-1889).

Damien was born Jozef ("Jef") de Veuster, the youngest of seven children and fourth son of the Flemish corn merchant Joannes Franciscus ("Frans") De Veuster and his wife Anne-Catherine ("Cato") Wouters in the village of Tremelo in Flemish Brabant of rural Belgium. Damien became a "Picpus" Brother (another name for members of the Congregation of the Sacred Hearts of Jesus and Mary) in 1860. Their special mission was to evangelize the Pacific Islands.

His superiors thought that he was not a good candidate for the priesthood because he lacked education. But because he had learned Latin well from his brother, his superiors did allow him to become a priest. Damien prayed daily before a picture of St. Francis Xavier, patron of missionaries, to be sent on a mission. Three years later, when Damien's brother, Father Pamphile, could not travel to Hawaii as a missionary because of illness, Damien was allowed to take his place.

It is believed that Chinese workers carried leprosy to the Hawaiian islands in the 1830s and 1840s. In 1865, out of fear of this contagious disease, Hawaiian King Kamehameha IV and the Hawaiian Legislature passed the "Act to Prevent the Spread of Leprosy." This law quarantined the lepers of Hawaii, requiring the most serious cases to be moved to a settlement colony of Kalawao on the eastern end of the Kalaupapa peninsula on the island of Molokai. Fr. Damien asked his bishop to go to Molokai to care for the lepers there. He told his bishop, "I know many of these unfortunate souls and I ask only to share their lot and their prison."

And a prison it was—a prison of degradation, suffering and death. During his time there, not only did Damien take care of the lepers, he also aided the colony by teaching, painting houses, organizing farms, arranging the construction of chapels, roads, hospitals and churches. He also personally dressed residents, dug graves, built coffins and lived with the lepers as equals. Six months after his arrival at Kalawao, he wrote to his brother, Pamphile, in Europe, "I make myself a leper with the lepers to gain all to Jesus Christ."

Father Damien told the lepers that despite what the outside world thought of them, they were always precious in the eyes of God. Under the leadership of Father Damien, laws were more strongly enforced, farms were more organized, and schools along with an education system were established. He set out to restore the dignity of these lepers. He organized them into work groups that constructed roads, cottages and clinics. He organized footraces, even for those who had lost their feet. He cheered the island by forming a choir and a band. Two organists who had ten fingers between them played at funeral Masses.

In December 1884, while preparing to bathe, Damien realized he had contracted leprosy after eleven years of working in the colony. He died of leprosy on April 15, 1889, at age 49. He was laid to rest under the same tree where he first slept upon his arrival on Molokai.

Damien de Veuster is another one of those Catholics who changed the world we live in. His life gave the world an incredible example of dedication to the most shunned people in our world and the most feared disease, leprosy.

23

Day, Dorothy: Social Justice

One of the buzzwords in modern society is "social justice." It is about fair and just relations between each individual and society. The term may be rather recent, but the idea behind it is not. The idea of social justice can be traced back to St. Augustine of Hippo, but the term "social justice" itself came in use from the 1840s on. A Jesuit priest named Luigi Taparelli is typically credited with coining the term. Pope Leo XIII (§44), who studied under Taparelli, made frequent use of it. Pope Pius XI used it frequently in three of his encyclicals, saying that society can be just only if individuals and institutions are just. Therefore, it should not be confused with "equal distribution of goods" or a "redistribution of wealth"—which is taking from the rich and giving to the poor—for that may not be just either.

Who played a key role in bringing this idea back into the minds of many Catholics? Arguably, one of the best candidates for this role is Dorothy Day (1897-1980).

Dorothy Day's life did not start promising for her future role. Day's parents were nominal Christians who rarely attended church. Yet, as a young child, Dorothy showed a marked religious streak, reading the Bible frequently. But then, as a young woman, she began living a bohemian lifestyle in New

York's Greenwich Village, drifting in and out of love affairs, and engaging in social activism as popular in socialist and anarchist circles.

However, her interest in religion began to grow. Soon after the birth of her daughter Tamar Teresa, on March 4, 1926, Day encountered a local Catholic Religious Sister, Sister Aloysia, S.C., With her help and to the dismay of her friends, she converted to Catholicism in 1927 and had her baby baptized.

In the 1930, Day came in contact with Peter Maurin, who was deeply versed in the writings of the Church Fathers and the papal documents on social matters that had been issued by Pope Leo XIII and his successors. Maurin provided Day with the grounding in Catholic theology of the need for the social action they both felt called to.

Though no longer a socialist, she was still deeply concerned by the plight of the poor, and so, along with Peter Maurin, she founded the *Catholic Worker Movement*, a pacifist movement that combines direct aid for the poor and homeless with nonviolent direct action on their behalf, thus putting Catholic social teaching into practice. When the Great Depression raged, they both set up urban houses of hospitality for the homeless and communal farms to grow food. Soup kitchens were founded where the hungry were addressed as "Sir."

As part of the Catholic Worker Movement, Day co-founded the Catholic Worker newspaper in 1933, and served as its editor from 1933 until her death in 1980. In this newspaper, Day advocated the Catholic economic theory of *distributism*, which she considered a third way between capitalism and socialism. The newspaper provided coverage of strikes, explored working conditions, especially of women and blacks, and spelled out papal teaching on social issues. The paper's principal competitor both in distribution and ideology was the *Communist*

Daily Worker. Day opposed its atheism, its advocacy of "class hatred" and violent revolution, and its opposition to private property.

In 1938, she published an account of the transformation of her political activism into religiously motivated activism in her book *From Union Square to Rome*. She presented it as an answer to Communist relatives and friends who had asked her, "How could you become a Catholic?" She answered: "What I want to bring out in this book is a succession of events that led me to His feet, glimpses of Him that I received through many years which made me feel the vital need of Him and of religion."

In 1972, the Jesuit magazine *America* marked her 75th birthday by devoting an entire issue to Dorothy Day and the Catholic Worker movement. The editors wrote: "By now, if one had to choose a single individual to symbolize the best in the aspiration and action of the American Catholic community during the last forty years, that one person would certainly be Dorothy Day."

Dorothy Day is another one of those Catholics who changed the world we live in. She was a social reformer who re-vitalized the idea of social justice and spread the Church's social teachings though her widely read magazine.

24

Dowling, Edward: Addictions

According to the news media—and this time, it's certainly not "false news"—our modern society is infested with addictions; so many are over-dosed, over-loaded, over-eaten and over-sexed. One of the oldest addictions is probably alcoholism; frequent drunkenness seems to be of all ages, as is perpetual drunkenness. And something similar can be said about many other addictions.

Have you ever heard of Matt Talbot (1856 - 1925)? At the age of twelve, Matt got his first job in Dublin, Ireland; it was in a wine bottling store, and that's when his excessive drinking began. From his early teens until age 28, Matt's only aim in life was liquor. One evening, when he was 28, he went out and found a priest, went to confession and "took the Pledge" for three months. Many times he felt he would not be able to hold out for three months, but within a year, he renewed the pledge for life, never touching alcohol again, for 41 more years.

Can the tide of addiction be turned? Matt Talbot turned the tide with a *pledge* which gave him the strength that comes from a higher power. Something like that can also be found in the Twelve Steps promoted by the organization *Alcoholic Anonymous* (AA). The first twelve-step fellowship was founded in 1935 by Bill Wilson and Dr. Robert Holbrook Smith, known to AA members as "Bill W." and "Dr. Bob", in Akron, Ohio. One of their core beliefs was that a Power greater than ourselves could restore us to sanity. Where the addicted person has lost the power to choose, another Power has to take over.

That's where Father Edward Dowling, S.J. (1898-1960) comes into the picture. Though not himself an alcoholic, he was a close friend and spiritual advisor to Bill Wilson, one of the two co-founders of Alcoholics Anonymous. The two became devoted, life-long friends, with Father Dowling in the role of spiritual advisor.

How did the two meet? It was 10 p.m. when the doorbell rang at Bill's department. The custodian said there was "some bum from St. Louis" to see him. Reluctantly, Bill said, "Send him up." To himself, he muttered, "Not another drunk!" But Bill welcomed the stranger all the same. As the man shuffled to a wooden chair opposite the bed and sat down, his black raincoat fell open, revealing a Roman collar. "I'm Father Ed Dowling from St. Louis," he said. "A Jesuit friend and I have been struck by the similarity of the AA Twelve Steps and the Spiritual Exercises of St. Ignatius" (§38). Bill answered, "Never heard of them." And they talked and talked the rest of that night. Thus began a 20-year friendship nourished by visits, phone calls and letters. From then on, Bill would turn to Fr. Ed as a spiritual sponsor, a friend.

When a drinking friend from Chicago lost his wife, Father Ed took him to a meeting of Alcoholics Anonymous, in those days a fledgling organization. Fr. Ed believed in the Twelve Steps of AA, given their similarity to Ignatian spirituality—surrender to a Higher Power, rigorous honesty, a daily examination of conscience. Later on, he said that a priest alcoholic, who had written on the Spiritual Exercises, first pointed out to him the similarity with the Twelve Steps of AA.

In 1942, Father wrote to Bill that he had started a national movement for married couples to help each other through the Twelve Steps—CANA (Couples Are Not Alone). He used the steps to help people with mental difficulties, scruples and sexual compulsions. Father Ed rejoiced that in "moving therapy from the expensive clinical couch to the low-cost coffee bar, from the inexperienced professional to the informed amateur, AA has democratized sanity." He invited people to be "wounded healers" for each other.

Since then the twelve-step methods have been adapted to address a wide range of addictions—alcoholism, substance-abuse and dependency problems. Over 200 self-help organizations—often known as fellowships with a worldwide membership of millions—now use the Twelve Steps for recovery.

Thus Father Ed endorsed AA for American Catholics. He was the first to see wider applications of the Twelve Steps to other addictions, and wrote about that in AA's magazine in its spring 1960 issue. Bill added a last line to that article: "Father Ed, an early and wonderful friend of AA, died as this last message went to press. He was the greatest and most gentle soul to walk this planet."

Fr. Edward Dowling is another one of those Catholics who changed the world we live in. He met the addiction problem head-on and helped millions of people, directly and indirectly. He changed the stigma of addiction.

25

Drexel, Katharine: Human Diversity

It seems to be part of human nature that we like to identify with groups of which we consider ourselves to be part: males or females, blacks or whites, New Yorkers or Puerto Ricans, Irish or Italians, progressives or conservatives, and the list can go on and on.

But making such distinctions obscures the fact that we all belong to the same human family: many races, but one human race. This is not only confirmed by science, but it's also the core of the Christian message: we are all children of the same Father. The "unity of the human race" is what might even be called an "indirect" dogma in Catholicism since it is presupposed by the doctrine of Original Sin—a sin shared by all of humanity.

Someone who broke through all the barriers of categories and divisions set up in humanity was Katherine Drexel (1858-1955).

Katherine Drexel was an American heiress, philanthropist, religious sister, educator and foundress. She was born Catherine Mary Drexel in Philadelphia, the second child of investment banker Francis Anthony Drexel and Hannah Langstroth. Mary's first year was traumatic; her mother died a month after her birth. After her father's remarriage, she and her

25 Drexel, Katharine: Human Diversity

older sister, Elizabeth, came home, and it would be years before the girls realized that their father's new wife, Emma Bouvier, was not their biological mother.

The Drexels were a French-Catholic family, deeply religious and intensely philanthropic. Katharine grew up seeing her father pray for 30 minutes each evening. Twice weekly, the Drexel family distributed food and clothing, and they gave assistance from their family home at 1503 Walnut Street in Philadelphia. Yet, the Drexels traveled a lot. When the family was visiting the Western states, Katharine saw first-hand the troubling situation of the Native Americans, who were then being forced from the rapidly shrinking frontier onto reservations. She desperately wanted to help them.

For that, she would need financial resources. Fortunately, Katharine's family was one of the wealthiest in America, and she was related to some of the most prominent figures in American financial and political history. Her grandfather partnered with J. P. Morgan to found the banking giant Drexel, Morgan & Co., later renamed J. P. Morgan. Her uncle founded Drexel University. So when, in 1885, Katherine's high-powered banker father died, he left behind a $15 million estate—in current dollars, the estate would be worth at least $400 million.

Katherine soon concluded that still more was needed to help the Native Americans—the lacking ingredient was people. So she and her two sisters travelled to Europe after their father's death, in January 1887, and were received in a private audience by Pope Leo XIII (§44). They asked him for missionaries to staff some Indian missions that they had been financing. To their surprise, the Pope turned the request back on Katherine: the missionary she needed, he suggested, was herself. And so she followed his advice and joined the Sisters of Mercy in Pittsburgh in May 1889. Her decision rocked Philadelphia's social circles. The *Philadelphia Public Ledger* carried a headline: "Miss Drexel Enters a Catholic Convent—Gives Up Seven Million."

When she professed her first vows as a religious, she dedicated herself to work among the American-Indians and African-Americans in the western and southwestern United States. She took the name "Mother Katharine," and, joined by thirteen other women, soon established a religious congregation, the *Sisters of the Blessed Sacrament*. Added to the normal vows of poverty, chastity and obedience, the Sisters professed a special vow, not to "undertake any work which would lead to the neglect or abandonment of the Indian or Colored races."

The bulk of the order's efforts went into developing a network of 145 missions, 12 schools for Native Americans, and 50 schools for African Americans throughout the South and West. By the time of her death, she had more than 500 Sisters teaching in 63 schools throughout the country, and she established 50 missions for Native Americans in 16 different states. Xavier University of Louisiana, the only historically black Catholic college in the US, also owes its existence to Katherine Drexel. In 1915, with a $750,000 grant from Drexel, the Sisters would found the University designed to train teachers who could staff the order's burgeoning network of schools.

Katherine Drexel is another one of those Catholics who changed the world we live in. She lived diversity in action, within one large human family, diverse in race and color.

26

Duhem, Pierre: Science Roots

Most people have this wide-spread impression that science has nothing to do with religion—that they are actually each other's enemies (§1). No matter how often the Catholic Church has tried to correct this misconception, it is still very much alive. It has in fact even become a growing anti-Catholic prejudice in media and academia. Fighting prejudices is hard to do. As Albert Einstein once put it, "It is easier to split atoms than prejudices."

Someone who fought this prejudice among scientists is Pierre Duhem (1861-1916)—someone from their own ranks. He was a French physicist, mathematician, historian and philosopher of science. He is best known among scientists for his work on chemical thermodynamics and his contributions to hydrodynamics and to the theory of elasticity. He is less well known as a philosopher of science, whose name became famous through the so-called Duhem-Quine thesis, which holds, among other things, that for any given set of observations there can be a large number of explanations. In a simplified example, if all I know is that you spent $10 on apples and oranges and that apples cost $1 while oranges cost $2, then I know that you did not buy six oranges, but I do not know whether you bought one orange and eight apples, two oranges and six apples, and so on.

Duhem began his education at a Jesuit school, the Collège Stanislas in Paris, where his science teacher had an important impact on his further life. In 1882, Duhem enrolled at the prestigious secular institution of higher education, the Ecole Normale Supérieure, where he received a degree in mathematics and another in physics at the end of 1884. In his final year, Duhem was offered a position in Louis Pasteur's laboratory as a chemist-bacteriologist, but he refused it because of his desire to work in theoretical physics. And when he was approached later in life for the newly created chair in the History of Science at the Collège de France, he again refused to be a candidate for it. The proud and stubborn Duhem told his daughter: "I am a theoretical physicist. Either I will teach theoretical physics at Paris or else I will not go there."

But Duhem did have one more remarkable interest: the history of science. When he studied the works of Catholic medieval mathematicians and philosophers such as John Buridan, Nicholas of Oresme and Roger Bacon, their sophistication surprised him. He consequently came to regard them as the founders of modern science since they had in his view anticipated many of the discoveries of later scientists. Thus he came to regard the medieval scholastic tradition of the Catholic Church as the origin of modern science. Duhem had to come to the conclusion that "the mechanics and physics of which modern times are justifiably proud [came] from doctrines professed in the heart of the medieval schools." Needless to say those schools were unmistakably Catholic.

Pierre Duhem did path-breaking work in the history of science when he showed that the doctrines of the Church have always been a permanent ally of, rather than an obstacle to, the success of the scientific enterprise in the West. He opened the eyes of many for the fact that it was actually the so often despised metaphysical framework of medieval Catholicism that made modern science possible.

Many historians of science and other scholars would later follow his lead. The sociologist Rodney Stark, for instance, argues that the reason why science arose in Europe, and nowhere else, is because of Catholicism: "It is instructive that China, Islam, India, ancient Greece and Rome all had a highly developed alchemy. But only in Europe did alchemy develop into chemistry. By the same token, many societies developed elaborate systems of astrology, but only in Europe did astrology lead to astronomy." So Stark had to come to the conclusion, "Science was not the work of western secularists or even deists; it was entirely the work of persons who were devout believers in an active, conscious, creator God."

Duhem made us realize that the Catholic Church and the scientific community have a long-standing relationship with each other, actually an existential relationship: without the Catholic Church, there would most likely not be any science. The case could be made that science, as we know it today, was born in the cradle of the Catholic Church, which might explain why it was not born anywhere else—not in China (with its sophisticated society), not in India (with its philosophical schools), not in Arabia (with its advanced mathematics), not in Japan (with its dedicated craftsmen and technologies), but on Judeo-Christian soil with Judeo-Christian roots. Whereas almost every culture or religion has given rise to inventions and some form of technology—for one doesn't have to be a Christian to invent the wheel—science and scientific exploration of the world around us were nurtured in a culture with a distinct Judeo-Christian tradition.

The idea that Christianity gave rise to science might be a surprise to many, as it was to Alfred North Whitehead's Harvard audience in 1925 when this famous mathematician and philosopher told them that modern science was a product of Christianity. They were shocked, probably out of mere ignorance. But the idea was not new, certainly not flimsy, and had already been noticed by Duhem. No wonder then that many scientists have thanked the Catholic Church for her support. The nuclear physicist J. Robert Oppenheimer—not a Christian himself—had to acknowledge, "Christianity was needed to give birth to modern science."

Even someone like the philosopher of science Thomas Kuhn had to say about Europe—without identifying its Judeo-Christian heritage, though—"No other place and time has supported that very special community from with scientific productivity comes." Yet, there are still many people who are not aware of these facts. The historian of science Edward Grant is probably right in stating that the gift from the Middle Ages to the modern world, and to science in particular, "is a gift that may never be acknowledged. Perhaps it will always retain the status it has had for the past four centuries as the best-kept secret of Western civilization."

Why was the Catholic Church such a fertile hotbed for the emergence of science? Well, in the Catholic mindset, the Universe is 1) the creation of a rational Intellect and 2) capable of being rationally interrogated. It is this very Judeo-Christian concept of a Creator God that makes science possible. Belief in a Creator God entails that nature is not a divine but a created entity; nature is not divine in itself, only its Maker is—which opens the door for scientific exploration. Without this belief, we would not be allowed to even "touch" the divine. A created world, by definition, is not divine in itself; it is other than God, and in that very otherness, scientists find their freedom to act.

A rational God has created a Universe that we can explore with our rational minds, made in likeness of God's mind. The Book of Wisdom (11:20) says about God, "You have arranged all things by measure and number and weight." Hence the only way to find out what the Creator has actually done is to go out, look and measure. It actually requires the "humility" of scientists to wait for and subject themselves to the outcome of their explorations.

It could also be argued that a tendency toward a different conception of divine causality, which distinguishes Judeo-Christian religion from other religions, is exactly what might explain why natural science improved in the West and weakened, or even was lacking, within the rest of the world. Because the Judeo-Christian God is a reliable God—not confined inside the Aristotelian box, not unpredictable like the Olympians in ancient Greece, and not entirely beyond human comprehension as in Islam—the world depends on the laws that God has laid down in creation. Faith in this one God changes the Universe, once inhabited with spirits, deities and goddesses, into something "rational." In the Catholic view, only God is the source of the order as well as the intelligibility of the Universe.

The only way to find out what this order looks like is to "interrogate" the Universe by investigation, exploration and experiment. The door for science has been widely opened ever since. It is through scientific experiments that we can "read" God's mind, so to speak. It is this Catholic understanding that the world is both good and intelligible to us that laid the foundation for science and for Western society to pass onto successive generations the scientific discoveries that were made. Pagan cultures, on the other hand, created a view of the world that inhibited scientific advancement, as they don't view the world as rational. They view things as being controlled by numerous, even whimsical, gods and magical powers. They don't view the world as something that is governed by laws of nature accessible to the human mind and waiting for discovery.

True, we cannot trace all these developments back to Duhem, but there is no denying that his research and books about the history of science directed the attention to something that had escaped the attention of scientists and scholars who were blinded by their own prejudices. He saw a link between science and Christianity that had escaped many others.

Pierre Duhem is another one of those Catholics who changed the world we live in. He made us see the world of science in a different light.

27

Francis of Assisi: Mother Earth

Our environment is constantly changing—there is no denying of that fact. However, as our environment changes, so does the need to become increasingly aware of the problems that surround it. The news on television, in the newspapers and on the internet makes sure we stay on top of it by constantly reminding us of environmental issues such as climate change, global warming, pollution, overpopulation, waste management, endangered species and so much more. Awareness about these issues is collectively referred to as "environmentalism," especially so in the United States, or as "ecology" in Europe—not to be confused with ecology as a science that studies the relationship between organisms and their environment.

The reasons why these issues have become so pressing are probably very diverse. But in general it can be said that, as people began to move to urban centers, they became disconnected from nature, and their ecological or environmental intuition was lost in the process. This urbanization, combined with new philosophical trends and material improvements, made man appear self-sufficient, almost god-like. As man began to lose understanding of his proper relationship with God, he lost also understanding of his proper relationship with God's creation.

Who can bring back this lost awareness of our connection to nature and to God's creation? The answer won't come as a surprise: that person is Francis of Assisi (1181-1226).

Francis of Assisi was born in Assisi, Italy, as Giovanni Francesco Bernardone, one of several children of Pietro di Bernardone, a prosperous silk merchant, and his wife Pica de Bourlemont, about whom little is known except that she was a noblewoman originally from the Provence in France.

As a young man, Francis led a worldly, carefree life. An early biographer said, "He squandered his time terribly." But he was miraculously converted to become a friar, deacon and preacher. He founded the men's Order of Friars Minor, the women's Order of Saint Clare, the Third Order of Saint Francis and the Custody of the Holy Land. Thus he became one of the most venerated religious figures in history.

Francis of Assisi had many gifts to share with us, but one of his legacies is his great insight that God reveals himself in the beauty and diversity of nature. Francis loved nature because he saw in it God's handiwork. Much has been written about Francis' love of nature but his relationship was deeper than that. We call someone a lover of nature if they spend their free time in the woods or admire its beauty. But Francis really felt that all of God's creatures were part of his brotherhood. The sparrow was as much his brother as the pope. Rather than seeing nature and its elements merely as inanimate objects to be used and exploited by us humans, Francis understood the whole world as relational—sister, mother and brother with God as Father.

It is difficult to think clearly about Francis of Assisi. The first thing that comes to mind is the gentle saint who preached to

27 Francis of Assisi: Mother Earth

birds, tamed wolves, and padded about in flower-filled fields basking in the love of God. Indeed, Francis was a great lover of God's creation, but that was before there was such a word as environmentalist. He exemplifies many of the best attributes of what it means to be an environmentalist today, but he was not an environmentalist in the modern sense of the word. For Francis, nature wasn't something to be controlled, nor was it something to be worshiped in and of itself as a deity, "Mother Nature." For him, nature is our connection to God.

Francis expressed this best in his famous Canticle:

Be praised, my Lord, through all your creatures, especially through my lord Brother Sun, who brings the day; and you give light through him. And he is beautiful and radiant in all his splendor! Of you, Most High, he bears the likeness.

Praised be You, my Lord, through Sister Moon and the stars, in heaven you formed them clear and precious and beautiful.

Praised be You, my Lord, through Brother Wind, and through the air, cloudy and serene, and every kind of weather through which You give sustenance to Your creatures.

Praised be You, my Lord, through Sister Water, which is very useful and humble and precious and chaste.

Praised be You, my Lord, through Brother Fire, through whom you light the night and he is beautiful and playful and robust and strong.

Praised be You, my Lord, through Sister Mother Earth, who sustains us and governs us and who produces varied fruits with colored flowers and herbs.

In a way, Francis was almost ten centuries ahead of modern environmentalists. And he was praised for it. On November 29, 1979, Pope John Paul II declared Francis the Patron Saint of Ecology. In declaring Francis the Patron Saint of those who promote care for nature, the Church recommends him as a guide for animal and nature lovers, environmentalists and ecologists.

Then during the World Environment Day 1982, John Paul II said that Saint Francis' love and care for creation was a challenge for contemporary Catholics and a reminder "not to behave like dissident predators where nature is concerned, but to assume responsibility for it, taking all care so that everything stays healthy and integrated, so as to offer a welcoming and friendly environment even to those who succeed us."

Francis was most honored by his namesake, Pope Francis. On June 18, 2015, Pope Francis published his second encyclical, *Laudato Si´*, which heavily built on Saint Francis. The title is drawn directly from the first line of Francis' canticle, and Pope Francis begins his encyclical with one of the verses: "Praise be to you, my Lord, through our Sister, Mother Earth, who sustains and governs us, and who produces various fruit, with colored flowers and herbs."

Through *Laudato Si´*, Pope Francis invites all Catholics

27 Francis of Assisi: Mother Earth

from every country of the world to take care of our Earth, to be more conscious of "our common home" and of how we, as human beings, are now accountable for it. He also motivates us to prioritize the way we interact with nature and "to be protectors of God's handiwork." With Pope Francis' invitation, the subject not only continues to be relevant today, but it is imperative that we reconnect with nature and become responsible stewards who care for our brothers and sisters—including our Brother Wolf, Brother Birds, Sister Water, etc., and our Mother Earth.

Pope Francis characterized the "exploitation of nature" as the sin of our time. Pope John Paul II had said already, "the ecological crisis is a moral issue." Many Catholics, unfortunately, conflate anyone who's concerned about creation with secular environmentalist movements. Unlike secular environmentalism, Catholic ecology is God-centered. As humans, we can reflect back on our relationship with God where other creatures can't. Unlike secular environmentalism, Catholic ecology is also human-centered. This differs from most secular environmentalists, who tend to look at human beings as just one species among many. They quickly run their logic to the point where the environment takes absolute priority over man. Modern pagan environmentalists worship Gaia but not the Creator himself. They tend to forget that nature is something that is not divine but was created by God, and that God made man after his own image and likeness.

Therefore, nature is a manifestation of the love and intentionality of God, the God that created all things and privileged mankind with the task of being his co-creators and the stewards of his creation. Since we are merely God's stewards or trustees, we have a grave responsibility to cultivate the earth, not destroy it. We should use it the way God has intended us to use it. One might even say that our failure to acknowledge God is the root cause of the ecological crisis. The person who stressed all of this as early as the 1200s is Francis of Assisi.

Francis of Assisi is another one of those Catholics who changed the world we live in. He stressed a part of religion that many religious people tend to neglect and are neglecting again and again.

28

Francis Xavier: Missionaries

The word "mission" comes from a Latin word that means "to send." It was first used by Jesuit missionaries who sent members of their order overseas to establish schools and churches. So originally it meant "a sending abroad of Jesuits." But the idea of "mission" is much older, of course. Jesus himself sent his apostles on a "mission" to make disciples of all nations (Matthew 28:19–20, Mark 16:15–18). The Apostle Paul, too, was a "missionary" to the gentiles around the Mediterranean (§52). The Apostle Thomas carried the Gospel to India. St. Mark preached the Good News in Egypt. According to legends, the Apostle Matthew may have ended up as a missionary in Ethiopia or Persia.

Ever since, missionaries are intricately connected with the Catholic Church. During the Middle Ages, Catholic missionaries such as Saint Patrick propagated learning and religion beyond the boundaries of the old Roman Empire. In the seventh century, Pope Gregory the Great (§31) sent missionaries into England. And as more and more parts of the world became known through explorers, the Church followed them with her missionaries. Perhaps the greatest and best known one is Francis Xavier (1506–1552).

Francis Xavier, S.J.—born Francisco de Jasso y Azpilicueta— was a Navarrese Basque, born in Javier (Xabier in Basque), in the Kingdom of Navarre (present day Spain). His father was a counselor and finance minister to King John III of Navarre. He was the youngest in his family and resided in a castle which still partially stands today. As the young Francis grew up, he was surrounded by war. Navarre was the target of a campaign by King Ferdinand of Aragon and Castile, and the kingdom was eventually conquered. When the war stopped and Francis came of age, he was sent to study at the University of Paris. During his stay there, he roomed with his friend, Peter Favre.

A new student, Ignatius of Loyola (§38), came to room with them. At 38, Ignatius was much older than Peter and Francis, who were both 23 at the time. Ignatius convinced Peter to become a priest, but was unable to convince Francis, who had aspirations of worldly advancement. Francis was a proud, autocratic, ambitious man wanting to accomplish great deeds in the world. When Peter had left to visit his family, and Ignatius was alone with Francis, he was able to slowly break down Francis' resistance. According to most biographies, Ignatius is said to have posed the question to him: "What will it profit a man to gain the whole world, and lose his own soul?" Ironically, in time, Francis would gain quite a bit of the whole world without losing his soul!

In 1530, Francis Xavier earned his master's degree, and went on to teach philosophy at the University of Paris. At the time, Portugal was colonizing India. The Portuguese settlers in India and elsewhere were losing their faith and Christian values. To restore these values, the King of Portugal bade Pope Paul III to send missionaries to the region. The pope asked the new order of Jesuits to take on the mission. Ignatius ultimately decided to send Francis.

Thus it became Xavier's dream to gain the whole world for Christianity, especially the Far East, more in particular India, Japan and China. He tried to do this basically in three steps.

First, India. Francis Xavier left Lisbon on April 7, 1541, along with two other Jesuits. As he departed, Francis was given a brief from the pope appointing him apostolic nuncio to the East. He devoted almost three years to the work of preaching to the people of southern India and Ceylon, converting many. He built nearly 40 churches along the coast. He set his sights eastward in 1545 and planned a missionary journey to Makassar on the island of Celebes (today's Indonesia). His mission strategy was simple. He would gather the young in a village and win them with songs and jingles about the faith so he could reach the village adults next. However, his success was limited because he mostly interacted with the lower classes, whereas his more successful successors, such as Roberto de Nobili, S.J., aimed at converting the noblemen first as a means to influence more people through them.

Second, Japan. In Malacca, Francis Xavier had met a Japanese man named Anjirō. He had told Francis extensively about the customs and culture of his homeland. Anjirō became the first Japanese Christian and later helped Xavier as a mediator and interpreter for the mission to Japan which now seemed much more feasible. On April 15, 1549, he left for Japan, accompanied by Anjirō and two other Japanese men. He had taken with him gifts for the "King of Japan" since he was intending to introduce himself as apostolic nuncio. Francis Xavier reached Japan on July 27, 1549, but was not permitted to enter any port his ship arrived at until August 15, when he went ashore at Kagoshima on the island of Kyūshū. As a representative of the Portuguese king, he was received in a friendly manner. For a long time, however, Francis struggled to learn the language, so he had less success than he had enjoyed in India.

Third, China. His growing information about new places indicated to him that he had to go to what he understood were centers of influence for the whole region. China loomed large, so it was Francis Xavier's great ambition to get permission to enter China as a missionary. Before him, the Roman papacy had sent several missionaries and envoys to the early Mongol Emperors ruling China at the time. But with the establishment of the Ming dynasty in 1368 and reestablishment of native Han Chinese rule, the presence of Catholic missionaries and of European merchants, such as Marco Polo, would come to an end. China seemed now closed territory.

Nevertheless, in late August 1552, Francis set sail for China and reached the Chinese island of Shangchuan, close to the southern coast of mainland China, some 100 miles south-west of what later became Hong Kong. Around mid-November, he wrote in one of his letters to Rome that a man had agreed to take him to the mainland in exchange for a large sum of money. However, Xavier died at Shangchuan from a fever on December 3, 1552, while he was waiting for a boat that would take him to mainland China. That was the end of his dream.

But not really, for a permanent mission would be established in 1601 by the efforts of another Jesuit, Matteo Ricci, who had been inspired by Francis. His whole approach was quite subtle, interesting the Emperor and the Chinese authorities in aspects of western technology and learning as a point of opening. Ricci would be the first European invited into the Ming-era Forbidden City in Beijing. In 1602, Ricci would publish his map of the world in Chinese that introduced the existence of the American continents to Chinese geographers. As a side note, in 1644, a German Jesuit, Adam Schall von Bell, was appointed Director of the Board of Astronomy by the new Qing dynasty. Jesuits were also given posts as engineers, musicians, painters, instrument makers and in other areas that required a degree of technical or scientific expertise.

Did Francis Xavier succeed in his mission? In general, he did, at least to a certain degree. Modern scholars place the number of people converted to Christianity by Francis Xavier around 30,000. More specifically, he achieved the following.

In India, Xavier was rather successful. India still has numerous Jesuit missions and many more schools, although Christianity is thus far a minority in the Hinduist country.

In Japan, he experienced several setbacks. Although his work in Japan was subsequently destroyed by persecution, Protestant missionaries three centuries later discovered 100,000 Christians in the Nagasaki area. Apparently, with the passage of time, his sojourn in Japan could be considered somewhat fruitful as attested by other congregations established in Hirado, Yamaguchi and Bungo. But most of all, Xavier had made it possible for his successor-Jesuits to get established there. Today, there are 200 Jesuit priests in Japan, the majority of them Japanese. They minister to parishes and run the flagship Sophia University in Tokyo and Elisabeth University of Music in Hiroshima.

In China, Francis never had a chance to enter the mainland, but he inspired, indirectly, many missionaries to work in China. However, most Chinese Catholics and their priests were forced underground and developed their own Christian culture. Estimates about the number of Catholics in China nowadays fluctuate around 10 million, but that number could be much higher because many of them are "underground."

Perhaps Xavier's biggest achievement was that he would inspire numerous future missionaries to do what he had done. His missionary work, both as pioneer and as organizer, is believed to have converted more people than anyone else has done since the Apostle Paul. His success also spurred many Europeans to join the order, as well as become missionaries throughout the world. Besides, he insisted that missionaries adapt to many of the customs, and most certainly the language, of the culture they wish to evangelize. And unlike later missionaries, Xavier supported an educated native clergy.

Francis Xavier is another one of those Catholics who changed the world we live in. He had a world-wide vision and wanted to make Christianity a world religion. He certainly left his mark on the world. We are still harvesting the seeds he planted.

29

Gonzalez, Roque: Jesuit Reductions

The terms "colonies," "colonization," and "colonialism" have become tainted in modern vocabulary. They come with a history that we no longer want to be reminded of. Colonialism practically ended between 1945 and 1975 when nearly all colonies became independent.

Yet, we keep colonizing the world, not with armies but with ideologies. Pope Francis speaks of "ideological colonization." He used this term to describe what he sees as a form of oppression of developing societies by affluent ones, especially the West, through imposing an alien worldview or set of values on poorer societies, often by making adoption of those values a condition of humanitarian or developmental aid. As a result, a new culture comes in and wants to make a clean break with everything that was there before, wiping away the cultures, the laws the values, and the religions of a people. It has become an invasion of secular values.

Colonization was certainly not an exclusively Catholic phenomenon; it is at least as old as the Roman Empire; it was done by Huns and Vikings; soon after, it would be widely practiced by Muslim countries around the Mediterranean; and more recently it was done by countries such as Protestant England and Protestant Holland, as well as by Catholic Belgium and Catholic Spain.

Arguably the worst example of colonialism is the colonization of the Americas. Though the Catholic Church was involved with colonization in the Americas—mostly through Catholic conquistadors and Catholic missionaries that accompanied them—she also made several attempts to counteract the effects of colonization, effects such as slave labor, poverty, racism, discrimination, diseases. One of the first ones to do this successfully on a more than local scale and in quite an organized way was Roque González, S.J. (1576–1628).

Roque González was born in the City of Asunción, now part of Paraguay, in 1576. He was the son of two Spanish colonists, both from noble families. In 1598, González was ordained a priest and, in 1609, became a member of the Jesuits, beginning his work as a missionary in what is now Brazil. He became the first European person to enter the region known today as the State of Rio Grande do Sul.

At a time when many Spanish conquistadors were brutalizing and enslaving natives in the Americas, Roque helped the natives become self-sufficient and free. He did so by founding what has become known as *Reductions*, which are settlements for indigenous people in South America created by the Jesuit Order during the 17th and 18th centuries.

Roque González was the innovative "social activist" who created the model for these avant-garde communities: independent village communities of Indians that excluded European settlers. They had an ingenious structure. Each village provided a house for widows, a hospital and several warehouses. In the center of the square, there was a Cross and a statue of the mission's patron saint. The reductions were ruled by indigenous chiefs who served as the governors, but under supervision of the Jesuits. The social organization was extremely efficient and so successful that reductions spread quickly with a maximum population of 141,182 in 30 missions in Brazil, Paraguay and Argentina; and a maximum population of 55,000 in Bolivia. Did they change the course of history? Not really—they were more and more considered a threat by the secular authorities. But at least they made the lives of thousands of Indians more bearable.

Back to González, the "mastermind" behind the reductions. In 1613, he founded a Reduction in San Ignacio Miní and in 1615 one in Itapúa, in the Argentine Province of Misiones. Then he had to move the reduction to the other side of the river. He also founded the Reductions of Concepción, Candelaria, San Javier and Yapeyú. Then, in 1628, Roque and two fellow Jesuits, Alonso Rodriguez and Juan de Castillo, started a Reduction on the Iijui River and another one at Caaró on Brazil's southern tip. Somehow, they roused the hostility of a local shaman who decided to kill all Jesuits. On November 15, his men tomahawked Roque and Alonso at Caaró. Two days later at Iijui, they stoned Juan to death. But that did not stop the expansion of other and new reductions.

Roque González is another one of those Catholics who changed the world we live in. He protected the colonized from the colonizers by setting up an ingenious, humane system for their protection. He was an early paragon to counteract both territorial and ideological colonization.

30

Greene, Graham: Novels

Novels have been written about various aspects of life. The nonfiction world is a rich source for the world of fiction. The world of Catholicism is no exception. The Catholic faith has been a tremendous inspiration for some novelists. Like Jesus used parables, these writers use novels to express some mysteries of the faith. In fact, novels written from a Catholic perspective have had a wide appeal. A few names that come to mind are Ronald Tolkien, François Mauriac, Georges Bernanos and, last but not least, Graham Greene (1904-1991).

Greene was born Henry Graham Greene in 1904 in St. John's House, a boarding house of Berkhamsted School, Hertfordshire, UK, where his father was working. He was the fourth of six children; his younger brother, Hugh, became Director-General of the BBC, and his elder brother, Raymond, became an eminent physician and mountaineer. His parents, Charles Henry Greene and Marion Raymond Greene, were first cousins, both members of a large, influential family that included the owners of Greene King Brewery, bankers and statesmen.

Graham Greene boarded at the school where his father was teaching and had become headmaster. In 1925, he went to

Balliol College in Oxford. After leaving Oxford, he turned to journalism—first for the *Nottingham Journal*, and then as a sub-editor for *The Times*. He had also started a correspondence with a girl, Vivien Dayrell-Browning, then 20 years old, who, five years earlier, had shocked her family by being received into the Catholic Church.

Greene—an agnostic at the time—wrote later in his autobiography, "Now it occurred to me... that if I were to marry a Catholic I ought at least to learn the nature and limits of the beliefs she held." Greene said a first step in the process was the day when, while attending a Catholic service, "I slipped a note into a collection box, asking for instruction because my fiancée was Catholic." It worked. Eventually, Greene was baptized on February 26, 1926, and they married on October 15, 1927, at St Mary's Church in North London.

In 1938, Greene left Europe for a trip to Mexico to see the effects of the government's campaign of forced anti-Catholic secularization. That voyage produced two books, the most important of which was his novel *The Power and the Glory*. It was Graham's most favorite novel. It is the story of a manhunt in the jungles and mountains of Mexico. The hunted person is the last priest in a State where religion is outlawed: an imperfect priest, prey to alcohol and lust, yet a humble man who loves God.

The novel became very controversial. In 1953, the Holy Office informed Greene that *The Power and the Glory* was damaging to the reputation of the priesthood; but later, in a private audience with Greene, Pope Paul VI told him he had read the novel, and added, "Parts of your novels will always offend some Catholics, but you should not bother." François Mauriac put the novel in a wider perspective with the words, "This drunken priest, impure, trembling in the face of death, gives his life without losing for one moment the conviction of his vileness and his shame."

Yet, criticism remained. One of Graham's critics is Joseph Pearce, who doesn't hesitate to say about this novelist, "He doubted others; he doubted himself; he doubted God. Ironically, it was this very doubt that so often provided the creative force for his fiction. Perhaps the secret of his enduring popularity lies in his being a doubting Thomas in an age of doubt.... Yet if his novels owe a debt to doubt, their profundity lies in the ultimate doubt about the doubt." We should not forget, though, that doubt is not the same as lack of faith; you can only doubt if you do have faith.

But such criticism can hardly wipe out all the praises coming from other people. Some say Greene's greatest achievement was to revive the sense of evil in the English novel, from which it had been absent for a long time. Graham's novels receive their dramatic power by recovering the religious element—the awareness of the drama of the struggle in the soul that carries the permanent consequence of salvation or damnation, and of the ultimate metaphysical realities of good and evil, sin and divine grace. His religious novels powerfully portray the Christian drama of the struggles within the individual soul from the Catholic perspective. And as the *New York Times* wrote at his death, "many of his deepest concerns were spiritual: a soul working out its salvation or damnation amid the paradoxes and anomalies of 20th-century existence."

More generally, it could be said that Greene's religious novels are so powerful because they play in a modern world that we, his readers, know all too well. His fiction is gripping because it grapples with faith and disillusionment on the shifting sands of uncertainty in a relativistic age. Greene depicts the world as Hell, since that is the first step of the argument of faith: if there is Hell, must there not be Heaven? His hope of Heaven depends on the reality of Hell. Strange as it may sound, he believes in God because he believes in Satan.

In the world that Greene depicts, suffering and unhappiness are omnipresent; and Catholicism is presented against this background of unvarying human evil, sin and doubt. As his friend and fellow Catholic novelist François Mauriac puts it, "We feel that this hidden presence of God in an atheistic world, this subterranean circulation of grace, fascinates Graham Greene."

What made it perhaps harder to appreciate Greene as a Catholic novelist is the fact that he made it harder for Catholics himself. In a 1967 interview for *The New York Times* in Paris, he said, "Only a few of my books have a religious emphasis—'Brighton Rock,' 'The Power and the Glory,' 'The End of the Affair,' and 'The Heart of the Matter'—but I don't consider myself a Catholic writer, but a writer who took characters with Catholic ideas as his material."

Greene may have strongly objected to being described as a Catholic novelist, yet Catholic religious themes are at the core of his four major Catholic novels, which are widely regarded as "the gold standard" of the Catholic novel. Perhaps a reasonable explanation for Greene's objection is that Cardinal John Henry Newman, whom Greene read closely, always insisted that Catholic literature should not be confused with theology. Perhaps Greene sought to avoid this confusion by reminding readers that he was a novelist who simply happened to be a Catholic.

François Mauriac, recipient of the Nobel Prize for literature in 1952 and often compared with Graham Greene as another modern Catholic novelist, gave us a good perspective on Greene's *The Power and the Glory*, when he said, "There is corrupted nature and all-powerful grace; there is the wretched man, who is nothing, even in sin, and the mysterious love which pulls him from the depths of his misery and shame to make a saint and martyr of him." Then he ends his assessment with the words, "Dear Graham Greene, ... Shadows cover all the earth that you describe to us, but what a shining beam cuts across them!"

This puts perhaps a different light on Greene's Catholic novels. In other words, Greene's use of blasphemy is never so much to abuse or ridicule as it is to reaffirm God. Even in all events, in failing his faith, he blamed himself, not the Faith. In "A Visit to Morin," one of his later short stories, a lapsed Catholic novelist describes enigmatically—almost as in a mirror—Greene himself:

I can tell myself now that my lack of belief is a final proof that the Church is right and the faith is true. I had cut myself off for twenty years from grace and my belief withered as the priests said it would. I don't believe in God and His Son and His angels and His saints, but I know the reason why I don't believe and the reason is—the Church is true and what she taught me is true. For twenty years I have been without the sacraments and 1 can see the effect. The wafer must be more than wafer.

Graham Greene is another one of those Catholics who changed the world we live in—at least of our view of the world we live in. His fiction may help us to better understand the nonfictional world of Catholicism. He somehow "evangelized" through his widely-read novels.

31

Gregory the Great: Papal Authority

When you ask Catholics where the pope's authority comes from, they will most likely answer, "From Peter, the first pope." That answer is certainly correct, but there is probably much more to it. The person who would, some five centuries later, consolidate the Catholic Church under papal authority was Pope Gregory (c. 540-604), who became almost immediately known as "Gregory the Great."

Gregory was born around 540 into a wealthy patrician Roman family with close connections to the Church. His father, Gordianus, served as a senator and for a time was the Prefect of the City of Rome. Although the Western Roman Empire had collapsed long before his birth, many ancient Roman families still commanded great wealth and influence in the city. Gregory was born into one such family.

It was happening in the midst of a turbulent time, though. When Gregory was only two years old, in 542, the Black Death swept through the region. About a third of the population in Italy was wiped out by the disease. In addition to the plague, enormous invasions were threatening Rome. History describes this period as the "migration of nations." In wave after wave, invasion after invasion, invaders streamed across Europe. They thundered down from the North, came up from the South, across from the East, and one by one they stormed the gates of Rome.

No wonder, Gregory's youth was a sad one. He himself tells us that, for all of his boyhood, Rome was under siege by one barbarian conqueror after another. Within a period of less than twenty years, the suffering city was taken and retaken six times. Roman senators and people alike were massacred.

During this period, Gregory would become the prefect of Rome before he was even 30 years old. But after five years in office he resigned, founded six monasteries on his Sicilian estate, and became a Benedictine monk in his own home at Rome, where he had the family villa converted into a monastery. He spoke later of these years as "the happiest portion of my life." He was ordained a priest and became one of the pope's seven deacons in the city. When word came that Pope Pelagius had fallen victim of the dreaded plague, the Church was left without a head, and Rome without a protector. After the first shock of the Pope's death, the eyes of the Romans turned to Gregory. At that time it was within the power of the clergy, the senate and the people to elect a new pope. And this they did without any hesitation in 590. They chose Gregory—much to his consternation.

Gregory saw for himself a double task as the new pope—establishing civil authority as well as spiritual authority. The first task was needed because Europe was experiencing a serious *political* unrest. It was a disintegrated West that needed new political and civil authority. Pope Gregory was the right man for it. Because of the sheer inability of the rulers of the Eastern Empire to assert any civil authority over Italy, and because there was no longer any military authority left in

31 Gregory the Great: Papal Authority

Rome, Pope Gregory was compelled to assume these tasks.

Besides, for a long time, the Holy See had not exerted any effective leadership in the West. The episcopacy in Gaul was ruled by powerful territorial families, and identified with them. Spain was ruled by Visigoths. The territories in Italy, which had been under the administration of the papacy, were beset by the violent Lombard dukes. In the midst of this chaos, Gregory founded the great civilization which has lasted down to our day and of which we are part, Western Civilization.

All alone, in the midst of famine and pestilence, floods and earthquakes, endangered by Greeks and barbarians alike, and abandoned by the Emperor of the East, Pope Gregory saved his people, his city, his country, Europe and the whole of Christendom. He had made himself the political leader of the West. For example, he unilaterally appointed governors in Italian cities. Under his guarding and administering hand, the "Rome of the Popes" rose up from the ruins of the "Rome of the Emperors."

And then there was the *spiritual* unrest that Gregory wanted to turn around. Not only had Europe been inundated by six barbarian nations, but it had also seen its orthodox Catholicism replaced by the cults of the pagan Anglo-Saxons in Britain, the pagan Franks in Northern France, the Arian Visigoths in Southern France and Spain, the Arian Ostrogoths in Italy, the Arian Vandals in North Africa and the Arian Burgundians in Eastern France.

He made every effort possible to root out paganism in Gaul, Donatism in Africa, and Arianism (§5 and §19) among the Lombards and Visigoths. Eventually, he would align them with Rome in religion. And his efforts were very successful. He recovered Spain from the Arians. He was able to begin the conversion of the Lombard nation and the tempering of their ferocious and cruel natures. He won France back from the bad spiritual state into which the country had fallen during the years which followed the death of King Clovis.

He also made it his mission to re-energize the Church's missionary work among the non-Christian peoples of northern Europe. He is most famous for sending a mission, under Augustine of Canterbury, to evangelize the pagan Anglo-Saxons of England. His influence in Britain was such that he is justly called the "Apostle of the English." The mission was so successful that missionaries from England would later set out for other pagan regions: the Netherlands and Germany. This was the first recorded large-scale mission from Rome, the so-called Gregorian Mission, to convert a pagan people to Christianity.

And then there was the contentious relationship with the imperial government of the East, centered in Constantinople. Gregory found a formula to deal with this relationship. He withstood the arrogant power of the Byzantine Emperor and looked upon Church and State as co-operating in a united whole, albeit with two distinct spheres, ecclesiastical and secular. Presiding over this commonwealth were the pope and the emperor, each supreme in his own department. Yet, he often would call in the aid of the secular arm to suppress schism, heresy, or idolatry. On the other hand, when the emperor interfered in Church matters, the pope's policy was to comply if possible, unless obedience was sinful.

Because of all of this, Gregory is rightly called the father of the medieval papacy. He claimed for the Apostolic See, and for himself as pope, a primacy—not of honor, but of supreme authority over the Church Universal. Gregory called himself the "servant of the servants of God." In the Eastern Churches, too, the papal authority was exercised with a frequency unusual

31 Gregory the Great: Papal Authority

before his time, and we find no less an authority than the Patriarch of Alexandria submitting himself humbly to the pope's "commands." From then on, Rome as the papal capital would continue to be the center of the Christian world. Gregory the Great was the first Pope to use the phrase, "to speak ex cathedra."

In short, Pope Gregory exercised in many respects a momentous influence on the doctrine, the organization and the discipline of the Catholic Church. He made himself the political leader of the West, rebuilt Rome, rescued its population from famine and plague, conducted a spiritual reform of the Church, withstood the arrogant power of the Byzantine emperor, initiated the temporal power of the papacy, stopped the Lombard invasions, sponsored the creation of "Gregorian" chant, and engineered the conversion of the English to Christianity. His achievements leave us breathless.

To him we must look for an explanation of the religious situation of the Middle Ages. Without him, the evolution of medieval Christianity would be nearly inexplicable. The influence of Gregory the Great was so widespread that the great modern scholar Henri de Lubac dubbed the period from Gregory's death up to the thirteenth century as "The Gregorian Middle Ages." The Anglican historian James Barmby put it this way: "It is impossible to conceive what would have been the confusion, the lawlessness, the chaotic state of the Middle Ages without the medieval papacy; and of the medieval papacy, the real father is Gregory the Great."

Gregory the Great is another one of those Catholics who changed the world we live in. He established for all time the power of the bishop of Rome, virtually founding the powerful medieval papacy. His legacy still surrounds us.

32

Gregory VII: Church and State

We live in a world that doesn't accept any interference of any church in any state affairs. In countries such as the United States, this principle has even been incorporated into the Constitution. It makes sense—the church should not interfere with state affairs. But also the opposite makes sense—the state should not interfere with church affairs.

This idea goes actually as far back as Jesus himself. What we call nowadays the separation of church and state is in fact Jesus' "invention." When Pope Benedict XVI discussed the separation of religion and politics—church and state, if you will—he wrote in his book *Jesus of Nazareth*, "In his teaching and in his whole ministry, Jesus had inaugurated a non-political Messianic kingdom and had begun to detach these two hitherto inseparable realities from one another."

However, this rather obvious rule got lost pretty early in Christian history. Very soon, when the Roman Empire had become Christian, the Roman Emperor would interfere with Church affairs (§0 and 19). The major fact of Church life in the early Middle Ages was that the affairs of the Church were managed by kings and princes. This interference in the Church's governance was actually seen as the king's duty. Like

32 Gregory VII: Church and State

the kings of ancient Israel, medieval kings were anointed at their coronation and invested with a spiritual as well as political mission. The historian Christopher Dawson once remarked that King Charlemagne viewed the pope as his private chaplain. It was the king's business to govern, said Charlemagne, that of the pope to pray.

In all of this, the Church had lost an important insight that Jesus had given her. It required someone of great stature to enforce this rule again—someone able and willing to fight with princes, kings and emperors who refused to surrender their power over the Church. This champion was Gregory VII (1020-1085).

Gregory VII was born Hildebrand in Sovana, now southern Tuscany, in central Italy. Some sources indicate he was the son of a blacksmith. He studied in Rome and became soon assistant to a few popes, and eventually treasurer of the Church. Elected pope himself, in 1073, Hildebrand took the name Gregory in honor of Gregory the Great (§31).

In that same year, Gregory VII issued *Dictatus papae*, which proclaimed the supremacy of the pope as the Vicar of Christ and the visible center of unity in the Church. He decreed that secular rulers could no longer choose bishops and invest them in their office. Many princes and kings simply ignored his order, but Emperor Henry IV of Germany opposed him violently. And this would start what would become known as the *Investiture Controversy*. The major issue of the conflict was whether it should be the pope or rather the monarch who would name ("invest") powerful local church officials such as bishops of cities and abbots of monasteries.

The conflict began with a dispute over the appointment of the bishop of Milan. King Henry IV had intervened to insure the consecration of his own nominee. So in a pointed letter,

Gregory reminded the king that he had no authority for such an action, and warned him that if he did not comply with the decree on lay investiture he would not only be excommunicated but also deposed.

Henry was infuriated and in response had "his" bishops renounce their allegiance to the pope. Once Gregory heard of this, he pronounced the sentence of excommunication against the king with all due solemnity, divested him of his royal dignity, and absolved his subjects from the oaths they had sworn to him. Once Henry's vassals (noblemen who rented the Emperor's lands) had been told they did not need to give their support to the emperor anymore, they staged a revolution. Now abandoned by his nobles and bishops, Henry decided to approach the pope as a penitent and ask forgiveness. In January 1077, in the dead of winter, he crossed the Alps, and after reaching the castle in Canossa where the pope was staying, the king stood barefoot in the snow for three days waiting to be received and given the conditions of his reconciliation.

Canossa has become a symbol of two people—pope and emperor, priest and king—meeting face to face, each testing the other who would blink first. Some would later invoke this symbol to make their case against the Church. During the conflict between Prussia and the Church in nineteenth-century Germany, for example, Bismarck is reported to have said, "We will not go to Canossa."

However, Canossa should not be misunderstood. The state does not have to bow before the Church—at least not in state affairs, only in Church matters. The pope's intention was only to reinstate what the Church had always said: We should render to Caesar what is Caesar's, but never should render to Caesar what is God's. Bishop Ambrose of Milan had said it very emphatically, some seven centuries earlier, during one of his famous sermons, "the emperor is within the Church, not above it."

Behind Gregory's action was a strong conviction of identification with Simon Peter, the head of the apostles. When his decrees were disregarded, Gregory said that Peter had been offended; he said about synods that the pope presides "under the power of St. Peter"; he said, when forbidding a candidate for bishop to accept the office, the pope does so "by the apostolic authority of St. Peter." Gregory's papal letters always stressed the role of the bishop of Rome in Church affairs. The Apostle Peter not only symbolized the unity of the Church, his authority also allowed the pope to govern as its head. And that's what Gregory did at Canossa.

However, Canossa would not be the end of the conflict. When Gregory refused King Henry's demands to crown him emperor, the king urged Pope Gregory to step down. As he put it, "Contrary to God's ordinance he desires to be king and priest at once." When the pope refused to step down, Henry pronounced Pope Gregory deposed, and named an imperial antipope, Pope Clement III, who reciprocated by crowning King Henry IV emperor. In return, Pope Gregory VII excommunicated both King Henry IV and Pope Clement III. The situation could not have been a bigger mess. When things returned to normal, Henry went to Rome and threw the pope out. Gregory was forced into exile and died in Salerno in 1085.

Did Gregory fail in his mission? Upon his death, there were few signs that his policies would triumph. Yet he knew the future belonged to him, and in his letters he seemed conscious his words would one day become authoritative. As a matter of fact, the controversy which had begun as a power struggle between Gregory VII and Emperor Henry IV, ultimately ended in 1122 when another emperor, Henry V, and another pope,

Calixtus II, agreed on the separation of church affairs and state affairs with the Concordat of Worms.

So it could well be argued that Gregory's actions had actually propelled the idea of the modern secular state. So far-reaching was his effect on society and so eventful his influence on the Church that many have called him a revolutionary. Following his dispute with Henry IV, he had been successful in deposing Henry, thus becoming the first pope to depose a crowned ruler. This revolutionary act affirmed the primacy of papal authority and led to the establishment of the new canon law governing the election of the pope by the College of Cardinals. The case could very well be made that much of the shape of modern Europe was determined by changes which had taken place in the time of Gregory VII.

Unfortunately, in the aftermath of the Protestant Reformation, the separation of Church and State, which Gregory had so strongly reconfirmed, was abandoned again for a while. As part of the Peace of Augsburg, in 1555, religious conflicts were suppressed by using a new principle—the principle that the religion of the ruler, either Catholic or Protestant, is that of the people: "Whose realm, his religion" [*cuius regio, eius religio*].

This principle was clearly contrary to what Pope Gregory VII had promulgated. Its disastrous effects would soon be felt in Europe. It made a legal division of Christendom permanent within the Holy Roman Empire, allowing rulers to choose either Lutheranism or Catholicism as the official confession of their states. The State was interfering again with the Church. Citizens who did not wish to conform to the ruler's choice were given a grace period in which they were free to migrate to different regions in which their desired religion had been accepted. And ultimately, it would motivate the Pilgrims to leave England in order to find "freedom from the State" in the New World. Soon, the US Constitution would reverse the course by enforcing "freedom from the Church."

Pope Gregory VII is another one of those Catholics who changed the world we live in. He separated State and Church and gave each their own autonomy back. He enforced what is considered standard nowadays.

33

Gregory XIII: Gregorian Calendar

When the world started the new millennium in the year 2000, we all did that on the same day. This was possible because we all follow the Gregorian calendar nowadays. It has a rule determining that years exactly divisible by 100 are not leap years, and this made some computer programmers assume the year 2000 would *not* be a leap year. However, years divisible by 100 are not leap years, with one exception: years that are divisible by 400. Thus the year 2000 was a leap year.

On each New Year's Day, too, just about every corner of the world will flip a calendar in accordance with the Gregorian calendar. Contracts, leases and birthday candle production all depend on the Gregorian agreement that the year begins on January 1 and lasts exactly 365 days, 5 hours, 49 minutes and 12 seconds. Even in cultures that maintain their traditional calendars besides, the smartphones will all tick over to the new year on the same day.

All of this is determined by the Gregorian calendar. But that calendar had not always been in effect. For many centuries, another calendar was in use, going back to the Romans and the time of Julius Caesar—the Julian calendar. Using the best calculations available, Julius Caesar extended the year to 365.25 days long and added at least 67 days to that year,

33 Gregory XIII: Gregorian Calendar

bringing January 1, 45 B.C. in line with the start of winter. And finally, to make the year as self-regulating as possible, he built in a leap day to recur every four years to make up for the ¼ day. Thanks to this calendar, historians are able to fix pretty exactly any event that occurred after January 1, 45 BC, although with some adjustment calculations. So one of the first accurate dates in Roman history is Caesar's own assassination on the March 15, 44 BC.

The Romans had not been able to calculate the length of the solar year with complete precision. So by the sixteenth century, the calendar year was ten days "slow"—that is, it was ten days behind the sun's position. Therefore, around 1560, the Council of Trent had required some reform of the liturgical calendar, and this would call for some corrections of Julius Caesar's calculations. These corrections were made by the Gregorian Calendar.

To whom do we owe the Gregorian calendar? Though he did not design the new calendar himself, the person who promulgated its introduction and use was Pope Gregory XIII (1502-1585).

Gregory XIII was born in Bologna as Ugo Boncompagni. He studied law at the famous university of his native city. At twenty-eight, he graduated as a doctor with sufficient distinction to become a professor of law in his own university. As a young man and a young professor, he was not very virtuous and had an illegitimate son. However, in 1538, he changed his ways and was ordained. From then on, his life was exemplary and notably austere. He attracted the attention of Pope Paul III who used his talents as a canon lawyer and made him a Cardinal.

Five popes later, upon the death of Pope Pius V in 1572, the conclave chose Cardinal Boncompagni, who assumed the name of Gregory XIII in homage to the great reforming pope, Gregory the Great (§31). It was a very brief conclave, lasting less than 24 hours. Unlike some of his predecessors, Gregory was to lead a faultless personal life, becoming a model for his simplicity of life. Additionally, his legal brilliance and management abilities meant that he was able to respond and deal with major problems quickly and decisively.

One of those problems was the calendar. Under Gregory's orders, an extremely accurate calendar was constructed, after being initially authored by the Calabrian doctor/astronomer Aloysius Lilius and aided by the Jesuit priest/astronomer Christopher Clavius who made the final modifications. The reason for the new calendar was that the average length of the year in the Julian calendar was too long, as it treated each year as 365 days, 6 hours in length, whereas calculations showed that the actual mean length of a year is slightly less—365 days, 5 hours and 49 minutes—that is, 11 minutes less than in reality. So the years in the Julian calendar were about 11 minutes too short, thus losing about three days every 400 years. To correct for this, the new calendar was going to eliminate three leap days every 400 years.

The new calendar was instituted when Gregory decreed, by the papal bull *Inter Gravissimas* of February 24, 1582, that the day after Thursday, October 4, 1582, would be not Friday, October 5, but Friday, October 15, 1582. Because of Gregory's involvement, the reformed Julian calendar came to be known as the Gregorian calendar. Proposals for replacing the Julian calendar with the new calendar were put to all the Catholic courts of Europe. The princes consented, so the October 4, 1582 was followed by October 15, and the Gregorian calendar was in force. It was a most impressive piece of international co-operation.

33 Gregory XIII: Gregorian Calendar

The introduction did not happen without controversy, though. The switchover was bitterly opposed by those who feared it was an attempt by landlords to cheat them out of a week and a half's rent. However, the Catholic countries of Spain, Portugal, Poland and Italy complied. France, some states of the Dutch Republic and various Catholic states in Germany and Switzerland followed suit within a year or two, and Hungary followed in 1587.

The non-Catholic countries continued to resist this necessary reform out of hostility toward the pope. More than a century passed before Protestant Europe accepted the new calendar. Denmark, the remaining states of the Dutch Republic and the Protestant states of the Holy Roman Empire and Switzerland adopted the Gregorian reform in 1700–01. The British and their American colonies did not like the idea of having their dates dictated by the Catholic Church and so stuck with the previous calendar makeover, the one done by Julius Caesar in 45 BC. They did not switch over until 1752, when Wednesday, September 2, 1752, was immediately followed by Thursday, September 14, 1752. Not surprisingly, there were riots in Britain that year by people who wanted their 11 days back. The last Protestant holdout in Europe to switch over was Sweden, on 1 March 1753.

For several hundred years, the Gregorian calendar was not accepted in eastern Christendom either. The Gregorian Calendar was only instituted in Russia by the Bolsheviks in 1917, with the odd result that the famous "October Revolution" actually took place in November. Romania accepted the new calendar in 1919 under king Ferdinand of Romania, so that November 1, 1919, became November 14, 1919. Turkey changed in 1923 under Atatürk, and the last Orthodox country to accept the calendar was Greece, also in 1923.

An added advantage of the new calendar, especially for the liturgical calendar, was that the date of Easter could be calculated more precisely. At the Council of Nicaea in 325 AD, the Church had fixed the date of Easter to correspond with the vernal equinox. There is a vernal (March) and an autumnal (September) equinox, which are the two times during the year when the sun crosses the celestial equator, and when the length of day and night are equal. The equinoxes are the only times when the subsolar point is on the equator, meaning that the Sun is exactly overhead at a point on the equatorial line.

However, thirteen centuries later, the date of the actual vernal equinox had slowly slipped to March 10, while the calculation of the date of Easter still followed the traditional date of March 21. In other words, the date of Easter kept moving further and further into the summer. Now that the Church had altered the method of adjusting the calendar, it could more accurately calculate the precise day of the vernal and autumnal equinox. The older Julian calendar was unable to fix the days of the equinox—a problem which had also annoyed scientists and agriculturists, who needed to know exactly when to plant crops at optimal times.

With the introduction of the Gregorian calendar, Western Christianity has Easter always fall on a Sunday between March 22 and April 25, within about seven days after the astronomical full moon. (The Orthodox Churches follow a different dating system and will thereby celebrate Easter one, four, or five weeks later.)

Everyone should be happy with the Gregorian calendar. It is almost perfect. However, some researchers have suggested that another tweak will be needed by the year 4000, when the Gregorian system will have gone off by about a day. But for the next 1,980 New Years or so, we should be able to make any

33 Gregory XIII: Gregorian Calendar

plans we like.

Gregory XIII is another one of those Catholics who changed the world we live in. Thanks to him, we're all "Gregorians" now, though it took a while for some to realize it.

34

Gutenberg, Johannes: Printing Press

Bibles can be found anywhere, printed and translated in many versions. So it is difficult for us to accept that a bible was hard to come by in ancient times. The Bible was on scrolls and parchments for a long time. Yet, for centuries, Catholics could not read the Bible because they could not afford or even get a copy of it.

During most of the Middle Ages, each bible was written by hand—another reason why the idea of everybody having a bible was out of the question, even if one was able to read. Since each bible had to be copied by hand, it took many years of a monk working behind the walls of a monastery, called a scriptorium, to do the copying. Each bible was made on sheep hide (vellum), so it took 250 sheep and thousands of hours to make each bible. That's why hardly anyone had or owned such a "bible"—it was actually sheer luxury.

This explains why copies of the Bible were chained to the walls of churches during this period—not to prevent people from reading them, but so that people could not steal them, or take them home to read, or take them away from others. So it is true that the Church did chain bibles to the wall in the Middle

34 Gutenberg, Johannes: Printing Press

Ages, but for the same reason that the Telephone Company used to chain its phone books to the booth: to prevent people from taking them away.

Apparently, times have changed dramatically. It's hard for us to imagine a world without printing presses, let alone photocopiers, emails and websites. Yet, for fourteen centuries, the world did not have such features. All of this changed dramatically when the printing press was invented. The man who made this revolutionary invention was Johannes Gutenberg (1398?-1468).

Who was Johannes Gutenberg? In spite of Gutenberg's importance, much of his life remains a mystery; documents about him are scarce and his name does not appear on any of the works printed by him. Although celebrated as occurring in 1400, even the year of Gutenberg's birth is unknown. Historical records do not reveal more than that his birth must have occurred between the years 1394 and 1404. His name Gutenberg was probably his mother's maiden name, or the name of her birthplace, or of land that belonged to her.

Maybe he attended one of the seminaries or convent schools in Mainz, as did most patrician children, and then later the university of Erfurt, since this was the alma mater of the Mainz Diocese. We think so because we can only assume that he would not have been able to complete his later achievement without a comprehensive education and a sound knowledge of Latin.

It's widely believed that as early as 1436 or 1437, Gutenberg and his partners had to be working on an innovative project: the invention of movable type (separate letters of the same shape). In the years 1452 and 1453, Johann Fust, or Faust—from a rich and respectable family of Mainz—loaned Gutenberg a good amount of money specifically for the production of books. With this capital investment, the type setting and printing of the Bible could begin. Between 1452 and 1455, in his two workshops in Mainz, Germany, Gutenberg used a system of individual letters and character pieces cast in metal that could be rearranged and reused in adjustable hand-molds. That's how he made the first printed book in the Western World—the so-called Gutenberg bible, also known as the 42-line bible. It has been acclaimed for its high aesthetic and technical quality. Each Gutenberg bible was made up of two books, the Old and the New Testament.

The print run was still surprisingly small. Gutenberg created between 180 and 200 copies of the Bible. Of these, it is assumed that about 150 were printed on paper, while the remaining 30 or so were printed on parchment. Forty-eight copies (36 on paper, 12 on parchment) still survive in Europe and American libraries; of these, one and a half are owned by the Gutenberg Museum in Mainz.

It is widely unknown that the first book ever printed in the West was not a Protestant but a Catholic bible. It was the Latin Vulgate Bible (§34) printed by Gutenberg. He printed his first bibles when the Protestant Reformer Martin Luther had not even been born yet. It is certainly no overstatement to say that due to Gutenberg, "the Word became print."

Johannes Gutenberg is another one of those Catholics who changed the world we live in. Thanks to him, all of us are able to have our own copies of the Bible, no longer chained to the walls.

35

Hieronymus, Eusebius: The Bible

Believer or not, no one can deny the influence of the Bible on Western Civilization. For a long time, the Bible had only been available in Hebrew, Aramaic and Greek. So for many people, the Bible would remain a closed book until it became available in a more contemporary translation. Since Latin was becoming the main language in the Western Empire, there was need for a translation in the "people's language."

Who would be able to take this enormous task on his shoulders? It had to be someone with a good knowledge of Hebrew, Greek and Latin. This person was Eusebius Hieronymus (c. 342-420)—better known to most of us as Jerome.

Jerome was born around 342 in a small town in Dalmatia, now part of Croatia. Although his parents were Christian, according to the custom then common, they did not have him baptized in infancy. When about 17 years old, he finished his education in Rome, admitting that worldly distractions had diluted his Christianity, but he finally cast in his lot with the Christian Church. He describes how on Sundays he used to visit, with other young men of like age and mind, the tombs of the martyrs in the catacombs, which culminated in his baptism at Rome. During these years, he acquired a considerable library, which he afterwards carried with him wherever he went.

Jerome is probably best known for his translation of the Bible into Latin—the translation that became known as the *Vulgate*. The Old Testament was written in Hebrew, but when more and more Jews in the Diaspora were no longer fluent in Hebrew, a legendary group of seventy Jewish scholars was commissioned in the 3rd century BC to make a Greek translation, commonly known as the *Septuagint* (Greek for "seventy"). The New Testament was mainly written in Greek as well. But when the division between East and West became more pronounced and an increasing number of Christians in the West were no longer fluent in Greek, several individuals had made Latin translations of parts of the Bible. In 382, Pope Damasus I commissioned Jerome to make a new and official Latin translation of the entire Bible.

Jerome was highly qualified for the job. In addition to Latin, he knew Greek and Hebrew well, which made him extremely competent to undertake such an enormous task of translating the entire Bible. Jerome spent forty full years working on his translation by using ancient copies of the Old Testament and from Greek and Latin manuscripts of the New Testament, many of which no longer exist today.

Jerome's translation had an enormous impact on Christianity in the West. It was the first complete translation of the Bible into the vernacular tongue of his day, which was Latin. This was to be the first time that the average man could read the Bible without having to be educated in Greek or Hebrew. At the time, the majority of people in the civilized West were part of the Roman Empire and consequently spoke Latin. The Latin used by Jerome was that of the common man, not that of the bureaucracy. True, not everyone could read Latin because for centuries there were no public schools and literacy was not that common, especially not among the peasants. But those who had been educated could read Latin. Latin was the common language of Europe for centuries; in fact, scholars and scientists published everything in Latin so that more people could read it.

The Vulgate's impact lasted for centuries. For quite a while, it would remain the only official Bible of the Catholic Church—with no other translation or version being considered its equal. Keep also in mind that the first book ever printed in the West was not a Protestant but a Catholic Bible—Jerome's Vulgate—a product of Johannes Gutenberg, the inventor of the printing press in Germany (§34). Even the first printed Bible in English was published by British Catholics exiled to France at the colleges of Douay and Rheims—and it was, as to be expected, a rather literal translation of Jerome's Latin Vulgate. They published the New Testament in 1582 and the Old Testament in 1610. This Douay-Rheims Bible went through several revisions. The entire project was completed in 1610, one year before the Protestant King James Version was published.

On a more technical note, many Protestants tend to look down on the Vulgate as an unreliable translation. However, it's worth mentioning that the Vulgate is quite a reliable version of the Bible because Jerome was able to base his translation on original manuscripts that are no longer available to us. During times of persecutions, in all parts of the Roman empire, Christians were decreed to surrender their religious documents. Although some of them handed over only heretical volumes or even medical books to police—making it look like they were obeying the edict—this was also the time when many valuable Christian manuscripts got lost for future generations.

On the one hand, thanks to Biblical research and

archaeological discoveries, modern Bible versions may have a certain superiority to older Bible versions such as the Vulgate. On the other hand, Jerome had still access to manuscripts that modern translators have no longer access to. Since errors tend to accumulate when the Bible is copied and translated, Jerome's sources could very well be more reliable than many of the manuscripts we have nowadays. In other words, these older, traditional versions bypass sixteen centuries of possible textual corruption. This leaves Protestants in the position of not always knowing if they possess what the Biblical authors originally wrote.

This explains why the Vulgate—and its English translation, the Catholic Douay-Rheims Bible—still has its own authority. For many Protestants, the King James Version (KJV) of the Bible has replaced this authority, but interestingly enough, the Vulgate translation was actually one of the sources used by the KJV translators to make their own English translation. One of the reasons was, as mentioned earlier, that Jerome's Latin Vulgate was based on original texts that are no longer available to us. In that respect, Jerome remains an invaluable link for Christianity, going far back to the early Christians. This means that although modern Protestants may have in some respects a "better" or more accurate Bible than their forebears, in other respects they may have a "poorer" or less accurate Bible.

An interesting case in this regard is the difference between the Catholic and Protestant versions of Mt. 6:9-13—of what Catholics usually call the "Our Father" and what Protestants typically refer to as the "Lord's Prayer." Both sides can pray together almost in unison during ecumenical events until they reach the end of the prayer. After "Deliver us from evil," Protestants always add an extra line, "For thine is the kingdom, the power, and the glory, for ever and ever." Protestant Bible

35 Hieronymus, Eusebius: The Bible

translations have this extra line in Mt 6:13, but Catholic Bibles do not because Jerome did not mention this line in his Vulgate translation. Jerome, and many other biblical scholars through the centuries, were of the opinion that, to the best of their abilities in researching the oldest copies of Matthew, this extra line was added by some pious translator to some very old translation of Matthew, but it was not there in the beginning. Therefore, it is not considered part of the Bible. No Christian wants to be at the mercy of translations and copies of the original made by people who had their own personal reasons for changing things. Not all sources are of the same quality; sometimes older texts may be more reliable than newer versions.

Perhaps one more misconception needs to be cleared. In the 5th century, when Jerome translated the Bible from the original languages into Latin, Latin was the language of the people. But when more and more people in the West were no longer able to read Latin, there was a growing need for translations in the vernacular. Although many think that such translations did not exist until the 16th century—until the time of the Protestant Reformation, that is—there were in fact some earlier examples. In 7th century Britain, before English was even a language, Caedmon, a monk of Whitby, paraphrased most of the Bible into the common tongue. During the early 8th century, Bede the Venerable (§7) also translated parts of the Bible into the language of the common British people.

As a matter of fact, prior to Martin Luther's Bible translation in German, there had been over 20 versions of the whole Bible translated into the various German dialects by Catholic translators. In Italy there were more than 40 editions of the Bible before the first Protestant version appeared, beginning at Venice in 1471; and 25 of these were in the Italian language before 1500—all of this with the explicit permission of Rome. These translators actually followed the example given to them by Jerome.

English translators of the Bible—such as Wycliffe's Bible, Tyndale's Bible, and the King James Bible—had to face an additional problem: Greek and Latin distinguish between you-singular and you-plural, while English does not. So they decided to use "Thou" for you-singular. This explains why God is not addressed with "you" or "ye" but with "thou" or "thee." It's not a matter of reverence. It makes for more accuracy: Jesus told Nicodemus, "I said unto thee [singular], Ye [plural] must be born again." (Jn. 3:7 KJV). What's in a word?

Jerome is another one of those Catholics who changed the world we live in. He was the first one to open the Holy Book for the Western World. We can no longer say we can't read the Bible.

36

Hildegard of Bingen: Using Talents

Not too long ago, a 112-year old woman was interviewed on radio. When asked what she considered the best invention during her lifetime, she answered without hesitation, "Running water." We don't know what it is like to *not* have running water. So I can feel how nuns felt in the 11th-century convent at Rupertsberg, Germany, when they were given fresh running water, one of the first examples of indoor plumbing in Western Europe.

The person who made this technical "miracle" happen in a convent of almost a millennium ago was a woman who was a fresh stream of running water herself: Hildegard of Bingen (1098-1179).

Hildegard of Bingen (German: Hildegard von Bingen; Latin: Hildegardis Bingensis) was born in the Rhineland in present day Germany as the tenth child of a knight. She became a Benedictine nun. In 1136, she was unanimously elected as superior of the community by her fellow nuns. Abbot Kuno of Disibodenberg asked Hildegard to be Prioress, which would be under his authority. Hildegard, however, wanted more independence for herself and her nuns, and asked Abbot Kuno to allow them to move to Rupertsberg. When the abbot declined, Hildegard went over his head and received the approval of Archbishop Henry I of Mainz. While Disibodenberg was in the hinterlands, Bingen was on the Rhine river, the busiest travel route through Europe. Hildegard clearly liked to be where the action was. Finally, Hildegard and about twenty nuns could move to the St. Rupertsberg monastery in 1150.

Hildegard had so many talents, too many to list. She was a visionary nun and a fount of knowledge, a polymath. She founded two monasteries, went on four preaching tours, composed an entire corpus of sacred music, and wrote nine books addressing both scientific and religious subjects, which was an unprecedented accomplishment for a 12th-century woman. Her prophecies earned her the title "Sybil of the Rhine." An outspoken critic of political and ecclesiastical corruption, she courted controversy. Here is just a short selection of her many talents.

The botanist: She is considered to be the founder of scientific natural history in Germany. She wrote books on natural history, reflecting a quality of scientific observation rare at that period. For Hildegard, the green of the leaves symbolizes a divine principle that gives all earthly lives the power and strength to thrive—the living bond between Creator and creation. She also discovered hops and is, consequently, the patron saint of beer—a staple in Germany.

The physician: Hildegard was an expert on the curative power of herbs, known today as holistic medicine. In her *Causae et Curae*, we find a list of more than 200 diseases and conditions along with herbal remedies for curing a number of illnesses. She made detailed studies of how to treat the sick. Modern herbal medicine practice has confirmed the healing

36 Hildegard of Blingen: Using Talents

power of many herbs described by Hildegard. Her work *Physica*, a medical textbook, was actually groundbreaking because it described also methods of healing women.

The advisor: One of the largest bodies of her letters (nearly 400) to survive from the Middle Ages was addressed to correspondents ranging from popes to emperors to abbots and abbesses. Hildegard corresponded with popes such as Eugene III and Anastasius IV, with kings such as Henry II of England, with German emperors such as Frederick I Barbarossa, and with other notable figures such as Bernard of Clairvaux, who advanced her work at the Synod of Trier in 1147 and 1148. Hildegard's correspondence is an important component of her literary output. In her letters, she spoke out openly against corruption in the Church. She was not a rebel or schismatic, but a woman ahead of her time who was deeply committed to the Catholic Church. That's why she crusaded against corruption in the Church and fought for reform of the clergy.

The feminist: Hildegard's influence came from her professional relationships and written correspondence with male leaders, including the pope himself. During her era, it was almost unheard of for a woman to exchange views and advice with such powerful figures. She could be seen as a "Renaissance man," though she was neither a man nor alive during the Renaissance, but was far ahead of her time. She also famously stated that "woman may be made from man, but no man can be made without a woman."

The artist: Hildegard also supervised works of art. Her "Universal Man" appears in one of the three volumes on her visions, which she wrote and illustrated. It is the first image of idealized proportions in Western art. She envisioned a series of concentric circles, including circles of air, ether, fire and clouds, and then a body appeared at the center. The body is proportioned as perfectly as Leonardo's—when superimposed, they are strikingly similar. However, Leonardo's famous "Vitruvian man"—depicting a man in two superimposed positions with his arms and legs apart and inscribed in a circle and square—was drawn more than 300 years later, around 1490. No wonder, Leonardo da Vinci listed Hildegard as their inspiration, and so did Dante.

The musician: During Hildegard's life, the dominant musical tradition for liturgical music was Gregorian chant. Hildegard composed her own music within this tradition, but introduced structural and tonal innovations. And while many liturgical chants were sung versions of the Old Testament psalms for monks to recite or sing, Hildegard also composed a wide range of new pieces, including antiphons, hymns and sequences of responses for the monks or nuns in community worship. All in all, close to seventy-five of her liturgical compositions have survived in musical notation with accompanying lyrics and poetic text. She composed also the liturgical drama *Ordo Virtutum*, "Play of Virtues," which is thought to be the oldest surviving morality play. It tells the story of a human soul's conversation with sixteen moral virtues.

A mystic: As she described it in an autobiographical passage included in her *Vita*, sometime around 1163, she received "an extraordinary mystical vision" in which was revealed the "sprinkling drops of sweet rain" that John the Evangelist experienced when he wrote, "In the beginning was the Word..." (John 1:1). Hildegard perceived that this Word was the key to the "Work of God," of which humankind is the pinnacle. Hildegard's most significant works were her three volumes of visionary theology. In these volumes, Hildegard first describes each vision she had, with details often seen as strange and enigmatic; and then she interprets their theological contents in the words of the "voice of the Living Light." Like all mystics, Hildegard saw the harmony of God's creation and the place of women and men in that.

A speaker: We have records of many of the sermons Hildegard preached in the 1160s and 1170s. She was a "public speaker," who travelled extensively and spoke on a variety of topics. The acceptance of public speaking by a woman, even a well-connected abbess and acknowledged mystic, does not fit the stereotype of her time. Yet, her speaking was not limited to monasteries; she conducted four preaching tours throughout Germany, speaking to both clergy and laity in private houses and in public, mainly denouncing clerical corruption and calling for reform.

A polymath: Like Leonardo da Vinci, she was a polymath—a person whose expertise spans a significant number of different subject areas. Far ahead of what would later become the ideal of renaissance humanists, she had a broad range of interests and talents. At a time in which women were invisible in intellectual and creative life, Hildegard was a composer, poet, philosopher, mystic, speaker, advisor, botanist and physician. And let's not forget about the monastery she founded—with running water!

Hildegard was unique because her influence came from her professional accomplishments, already recognized in her day. There were, of course, other women who were running convents of nuns, but Hildegard's writing, composition and public speaking gave her visibility and earned her recognition far beyond other women of her era. Nearly five hundred years before Gutenberg's press revolutionized book publishing, Hildegard's prolific writing on theology and natural science, as well as her musical compositions, were widely copied and read. She was a "woman for all seasons."

Hildegard was one of the first persons for whom the Roman canonization process was officially applied, but the process took so long that four attempts at canonization were not completed and she remained at the level of beatification. But in 2012, she was canonized as a Saint, and on October 7, 2012, Pope Benedict XVI named her a Doctor of the Church—the fourth woman of 35 saints given that title by the Catholic Church. He called her "perennially relevant" and "an authentic teacher of theology and a profound scholar of natural science and music." He also praised the "rich theological content" of her mystical visions that sum up the history of salvation from creation to the end of time.

Hildegard is another one of those Catholics who changed the world we live in. In so many areas, she was a first.

37

Ignatius of Antioch: Catholic or Christian?

Catholics usually call themselves "Catholic" to distinguish themselves from Protestants. And Protestants like to call themselves "Christian" to distinguish themselves from Catholics. This raises the question: Aren't they all Christians? As a matter of fact, the Apostle Paul started his missionary travels in Antioch in Syria, where the name "Christians" was coined— "believers in Christ." As the Acts of the Apostles tells us, "it was in Antioch that the disciples were first called Christians" (Acts 11:26). So shouldn't we all be called "Christians" if we want to be followers of Jesus the Christ?

How come some Christians still prefer to call themselves "Catholics" instead of "Christians"? That must have been a later invention, you might think. Where did that new term come from? To find out, we need to go back to Ignatius of Antioch (35-108).

Ignatius of Antioch was one of the first so-called Church Fathers, born around the time that Jesus was crucified. He was the Apostle Peter's second successor as leader of the Church in Antioch. He piloted his Church for over thirty stormy years of persecution up to his final journey to martyrdom in Rome. Although his road to martyrdom is probably the most heroic part of his Christian life, his letters are an equally heroic testimony of his Christian Faith.

In a farewell letter, which he wrote to his fellow Christians in Smyrna (today Izmir in modern Turkey), Ignatius made the first written mention in history of "the *Catholic Church.*" In his own words, "Wherever the bishop shall appear, there let the multitude [of the people] also be; even as, wherever Jesus Christ is, there is the *Catholic* Church." Thus, the second century of Christianity had scarcely begun when the term "Catholic Church" was already in use.

Given the casual way Ignatius uses the term "Catholic," without any further explanation, tells us he expects his readers to know it already as an accepted term. So he most likely didn't coin the term himself. For Ignatius and his fellow Christians, "Catholic" means that the Church is more than a collection of isolated and disconnected congregations. It is not a regional cult but intended to include all people of the entire world—global and universal, that is. That's why and how the term ended up in the Nicene Creed: "We believe in one holy catholic and apostolic Church."

The Greek adjective *katholikos* is a contraction of *kata* and *holos*, which means "about the whole," in short "universal." When employing the term at the time of early Christianity, Ignatius of Antioch was referring to the Church that was already "everywhere," as distinguished from whatever sects, schisms, or splinter groups might have popped up here and there, in opposition to the Universal Church. So it is actually a very appropriate term, as long as this doesn't mean that Catholics are not "Christian" in the sense of followers of Christ. In fact, they are both—both "Christian" and "Catholic." From

37 Ignatius of Antioch: Catholic or Christian?

very early history on, Catholics are Christians, and Christians are Catholics.

Indeed, Catholics are supposed to be Christians. However, in many people's minds, to be a Christian is often taken to be a Protestant. One could even make the case that certain Protestant groups have hijacked the term "Christian" as a tag exclusively for them. This is especially true in the Deep South of the USA, where you can hear people say, after they have left the Catholic Church, that they are no longer Catholic but Christian. The pernicious idea behind this is that Catholics are not Christians but rather devotees of a cult similar to Jehovah's Witnesses or Mormons.

In fact, it is equally true that Christians are supposed to be Catholics—members of Jesus' universal, unified Church. However, the term "Catholic" went through a change, too. In the New Testament, the Church is simply called "the Church." There was only one! There were not yet any break-away groups substantial enough to be distinguished from "the Church." But since the Protestant Reformation there have been serious break-away attempts from the one Catholic Church, which forced some to speak of "the *Roman* Catholic Church" to distinguish her from other Christian churches. Yet, the Catholic Church never speaks of herself as "the Roman Catholic Church." Nowhere in the 16 documents of the Second Vatican Council, for instance, will you find the term "Roman Catholic." There are references to the Roman curia, the Roman missal, the Roman rite, etc., but when the adjective "Roman" is applied to the Church herself, it refers only to the Diocese of Rome! Christians are Catholics.

Ignatius of Antioch is another one of those Catholics who changed the world we live in. Jesus founded the Church, but Ignatius made sure she was and remained a Catholic Church.

38

Ignatius of Loyola: God's Soldiers

The term "Jesuits" is probably known to most people, but they diverge greatly in what they think the term stands for. They may vary even more in how to assess those who are called Jesuits. Some of their critics have consigned them to the lower regions of hell. Some of their supporters have praised them to the higher reaches of heaven. No matter what, Jesuits are arguably a very controversial company of men in Church history. How did they come to be Jesuits?

The man who founded them was Ignatius of Loyola (1491-1555). Born in the Basque province of Guipúzcoa in northern Spain, Ignatius was the youngest of five sisters and eight brothers. Basques are known for their stubborn independence; Jean-Jacques Rousseau once called them "our guest aliens in the household of Europe."

Ignatius was known at the time as Iñigo Lopez de Oñaz y Loyola. His life of sixty-five years can be compartmentalized in four sections: a period of twenty-nine years during which he led a wild life; an eight year period of repentance; a period of study and preparation that lasted twelve years; and, finally, the fifteen years it took him to establish what came to be called the "Society of Jesus."

38 Ignatius of Loyola: God's Soldiers

After a pilgrimage to Jerusalem, he started the third period of his life. He decided to become a priest; for this, he needed to study. He entered a school in Barcelona to sit with boys less than half his age in order to study Latin, then threw himself into a dizzying year of courses at the University of Alcalá. But soon after, he made his way to the largest and most renowned university of his day, in Paris, where he changed his name to Ignatius, the closest Latin equivalent of the Basque name Iñigo.

By the time he finished his studies and left Paris in April of 1535, Ignatius had developed a quite defined and definitive vision of the world around him: there was a war in progress—not a local war between Christians and Muslims, not a war between Catholics and Protestants, but a universal war waged by Lucifer against Christ and his grace and salvation. So, for him to join the warfare on the side of Christ, he would need a team of like-minded men working for the same goals as he.

For this purpose, he had gathered a basic group of seven devoted companions around him. On August 15, 1534, Ignatius of Loyola, and six other students at the University of Paris, met in Montmartre outside Paris, in a crypt beneath the church of Saint Denis, now Saint Pierre de Montmartre. They called themselves the *Company of Jesus*, and also "Amigos en El Señor" or "Friends in the Lord" because they felt "they were placed together by Christ." The name passed through the Latin *Societas Jesu* and came out the other end as Society of Jesus—also nicknamed by most people as the Jesuits. The world was ready for them, but did not know it yet.

The first Jesuits concentrated on a few key activities. First, they founded schools throughout Europe. Jesuit teachers were rigorously trained in both classical studies, philosophy, and theology, and their schools reflected this. Second, they sent out missionaries across the globe to evangelize those peoples who had not yet heard the Gospel, while founding missions in widely diverse regions, such as modern-day Paraguay, Japan, Ontario and Ethiopia. Finally, though not initially formed for the purpose, they aimed to stop Protestantism from spreading and to preserve communion with Rome and the successor of the Apostle Peter. The driving motto behind all these activities was "To the Greater Glory of God" (*Ad Majorem Dei Gloriam*).

Ignatius wanted his men to be "all things to all men." And they certainly would fulfill that mission. There was no continent they did not reach, no known language they did not speak, no culture they did not penetrate, no branch of learning and science they did not explore. Already before Ignatius' death in 1556, the Order had over one hundred houses in twelve different regions of the world. Besides, Ignatius had founded thirty-five colleges for higher education. Jesuits worked in places as widely separate as Japan and Brazil. The Dutchman Pieter de Houndt, better known by the Latin form of his name, Peter Canisius (§14), was sent by Ignatius to Germany, Austria and Hungary, where he reclaimed whole provinces from Protestantism, founded several Jesuit colleges, and left behind him 1110 Jesuits when he died. The vision Ignatius had nurtured proved more powerful than anyone could have ever anticipated. It could be said that Ignatius had created a Catholic "empire" on which the sun never set.

Even after Ignatius' death, his Society kept growing and growing, not only in size but also in diversity. As God's soldiers, Jesuits developed a baffling and diverse fraternity. Not only are they now astronomers, psychiatrists, seismologists, engineers, biologists, theologians, lawyers, economists, but also teachers, parish priests, missionaries and martyrs. Let's just focus on their educational achievements first.

The Society of Jesus has a strong educational focus. The

Jesuits' standardized curriculum and teaching methods are still the basis of many education systems to this very day. Right now, the Jesuits still operate one of the most prestigious privately run school networks in the world, with more than 400 high schools and universities on six continents, including 52 high schools and 28 colleges in the U.S. The Jesuit colleges in the U.S. have become very successful. Going by enrollment numbers, Fordham has the highest (16,009), followed by Loyola University Chicago (15,545), Boston College (14,395), Georgetown University (14,148) and Saint Louis University (11,823). If one goes by applications, Fordham receives about 24,000 applications each year, Georgetown receives around 19,000, and Boston College gets 16,000, making them the three most popular in that respect. In terms of all those factors together plus selectivity, Georgetown would be the tops, though Boston College comes close. Although much smaller than the others, the Jesuit College of the Holy Cross is considered one of the best colleges in the country. There's also Marquette, which is not quite as selective as some of the other big universities but is still hugely popular.

Let's briefly focus on their scientific achievements next. Jesuit scientists contributed to the development of pendulum clocks, barometers, reflecting telescopes and microscopes, and have been active in scientific fields as various as magnetism, optics and electricity. They observed, in some cases before anyone else, the colored bands on Jupiter's surface, the Andromeda nebula and Saturn's rings. They theorized about the circulation of the blood (independently of Harvey), the way the moon affected the tides and the wave-like nature of light. In addition, their contribution to the study of earthquakes has seismology labeled the "Jesuit science."

Here are some famous Jesuit scientists by name. The

astronomer Christopher Clavius (1538-1612) modified the proposal of the modern Gregorian calendar after the death of its primary author, Aloysius Lilius (§33). Christian Mayer (1719-1783), a Czech astronomer known for his pioneering study of binary stars; Roger Joseph Boscovich (1711–1787), a Croatian polymath famous for his atomic theory; Maximilian Hell (1720-1792), a Hungarian Jesuit who wrote astronomy tables and observed the transit of Venus; Franz de Paula Triesnecker (1745-1817), an Austrian astronomer; Angelo Secchi (1818-1878), an Italian astronomer who drew an early map of Mars; Joseph Bayma (1816-1892), an Italian mathematician who did work relating to stereochemistry; Benito Viñes (1837-1893), a Spanish scientist who did research on hurricanes; Gyula Fényi (1845-1927), a Hungarian astronomer noted for his observations of the Sun; James Cullen (1867-1933), an Irish mathematician, known for the Cullen numbers; Theodor Wulf (1868-1946), a German physicist who was among the first to detect excess atmospheric radiation; James Macelwane (1883-1956), an American seismologist; Roberto Busa (1913-2011), an Italian pioneer in the usage of computers for linguistic and literary analysis; Kevin T. FitzGerald (1955-), an American molecular biologist; and the list could go on and on.

Obviously, the global impact of Ignatius and his "soldiers" has been enormous. Vladimir Ilyich Lenin, the founder of the Soviet Union, swore at the end of his life that if he had had twelve men like one of those early Jesuits, his Communism would have swept the world. Then there was Reichsführer Heinrich Himmler in Nazi Germany, who assembled an extensive library about the Jesuit order so he could train his Waffen SS combat troops along Jesuit lines. He even considered to have the principal officers undergo a form of

Ignatius' *Spiritual Exercises*—what a travesty! The plan never succeeded, but even Adolf Hitler joked about Himmler as "our very own Ignatius Loyola." That's certainly not a compliment for Ignatius, but it tells us how successful his work has been. We could hardly imagine the world today without his impact.

Ignatius of Loyola is another one of those Catholics who changed the world we live in. He gave his "soldiers" a worldwide mission. Directly, and through his followers indirectly, he has left heavy footprints behind on this earth.

39

Isidore of Seville: Schooling

Kids often dream of days with no school or of places without schools. But if those dreams would really come true, that would create a nightmare. People who cannot read or write and cannot perform basic calculations can hardly survive in modern society. Illiteracy is not only a menace to individuals but also to society at large. That's why most countries require a minimum number of years in school or in home schooling. And after that period, many still want to continue schooling and education by going to vocational schools or colleges. But even that's not the end. Many continue studying and attend evening classes or on-line classes. The latest trend now is "continuing education"—for, in essence, schooling and education never end. This has made us a highly educated lot.

We take it easily for granted that everyone has access to schooling and education, but the institutions which give us that opportunity didn't just come from nowhere. Someone had to implement some educational system somewhere. A key player in this process was Isidore of Seville (560-636).

Isidore was born in Cartagena, but his family migrated to Seville in Spain when he was young. That's where Isidore received his education, most in particular at the Cathedral

39 Isidore of Seville: Schooling

school in Seville, which was the first school of its kind in Spain, where he was taught the classic liberal arts—the *trivium* (grammar, logic and rhetoric) and the *quadrivium* (geometry, arithmetic, astronomy and music).

When his brother Leander died around the year 600, Isidore succeeded him as Seville's archbishop. Isidore inherited his brother's responsibility for Church affairs in an intense period of change, as the institutions of the Western Roman Empire gave way to the culture of the barbarian tribes. At a time of violence, illiteracy and disintegration of classical culture, Isidore was determined to stop this process. He did so by using educational institutions to counteract the increasingly influential Gothic barbarism throughout his diocese. His quick spirit animated a powerful educational movement that would rapidly spread from Seville to the rest of Europe.

What probably motivated him was what he had experienced as a young boy. Frustrated by his inability to learn as fast as his brother wanted, and hurt by his brother's treatment, Isidore ran away from school. When he sat down on the side of the road near a spring, he noticed a rock that had been hollowed out by drips of water—by the power of repeated and prolonged action. After seeing this, he decided to return to school and apply this same perseverance to his studies. Instead of running away from learning, he embraced education and made it his life's work. Isidore rose above his past, and in doing so, he became known as the greatest teacher in Spain.

It was through Isidore's influence that the Council of Toledo promulgated a decree, commanding all bishops to establish schools in their cathedral cities along the lines of the cathedral school at Seville, which had educated Isidore decades earlier. Reflecting Isidore's broad interests, the schools were to teach every branch of knowledge, including the liberal arts, medicine, law, Hebrew and Greek. The authority of the Council made this education policy obligatory upon all bishops of Spain. This way, the country was to serve as a guide for other European countries whose culture was threatened also by barbarian invaders.

But Isidore's influence went even further. He wrote a book, called *Etymologies,* in which he attempted to set down, in twenty volumes, the basics of all that was known on a vast range of topics, including grammar, rhetoric and logic; arithmetic, geometry and astronomy; law, military science and theology; cosmology; and agriculture, mineralogy, physiology and zoology, among others. Published after his death in 636, it was for almost thousand years considered the encyclopedia of all human knowledge. Written in simple language, it was all one needed in order to have access to everything one wanted to know about the world but never dared to ask—similar to what we do now through the internet. This explains why Pope John Paul II, when he wanted a patron saint for internet use, chose Isidore.

Everything Isidore did was propelled by his love of learning. No wonder, he is often called "The Schoolmaster of the Middle Ages" because his encyclopedia was used as a "textbook" for nine centuries to come. With his books and his educational system, Isidore helped shape the culture of Europe, and so, of Western civilization.

Isidore is another one of those Catholics who changed the world we live in. He laid the foundation for education in the West. Who knows what would have come of Europe without his contribution?

40

John Paul II: Communism

A word that we use over and over again is "society," but what we mean by it is not quite clear. Some see society as something that doesn't really exist. Looking around us, we perceive only individual human beings, but no such thing as a society. One never encounters a society as such: it cannot be situated anywhere; there does not seem to be such a "thing" in the world. The term "society" seems to be just a simple collective term for all, or certain, people combined. This makes some say that "society" is a pure fiction. The problem with this view is that it can't explain the evident fact that there is some kind of pressure society seems to exert on each one of us, at least in the form of customs, etiquette, civil laws and the like.

No wonder, this makes some go to the other extreme. They claim instead that society is the one and only real entity. Human beings are seen only as parts of a larger whole, and therefore do not qualify as complete entities. Just like the hand of a person is not complete in itself, but is only a part of the person, in the same way an individual person is only a part of society. As a consequence, individuals have no rights and duties of their own. After all, they live their lives as part of society, through the power of society, and for the benefit of society.

They live their lives in the same way as termites exist only to keep the colony alive. Obviously, at the very moment we glorify the "colony" over the "termites," individuals lose all their rights and become enslaved to the "rights" of the totality—which is pure totalitarianism.

Both views are extreme, of course. There must be a middle ground. Philosophers and politicians have come up with various ideas. But ideas are just that—ideas. What we need instead, or in addition, are actions. One of the best examples of someone who put ideas about society into action is Pope John Paul II (1920-2005).

John Paul II was born in the Polish town of Wadowice as Karol Józef Wojtyła. He was the youngest of three children born to Karol Wojtyła, an ethnic Pole, and Emilia Kaczorowska, whose mother's maiden surname was Scholz. Emilia, who was a schoolteacher, died in childbirth in 1929 when Wojtyła was only eight years of age.

In mid-1938, Wojtyła and his father left Wadowice and moved to Kraków, where he enrolled at the Jagiellonian University. He performed with various theatrical groups and worked as a playwright. During this time, his talent for language blossomed, and he learned as many as 12 languages—Polish, Latin, Italian, Spanish, Portuguese, French, English, German, Ukrainian, Serbo-Croatian, Slovak and Esperanto, nine of which he used extensively when he became pope. The school was closed the next year by Nazi troops during the German occupation of Poland.

Wanting to become a priest, Karol began studying at a secret seminary run by the archbishop of Krakow. After World War II had ended, he finished his religious studies at a Krakow seminary and was ordained in 1946. He became the bishop of Ombi in 1958 and the archbishop of Krakow in 1964. He was made a cardinal by Pope Paul VI in 1967, and in 1978 became the first non-Italian pope in more than 400 years.

As pontiff he had an enormous influence on the world. But perhaps his most important action on the world scene was his role in bringing down Communism in Central and Eastern Europe. He was the spiritual inspiration behind its downfall. The pope, who began his papacy when the Soviet regime was still in control of his native country of Poland as well as of the rest of Central and Eastern Europe, was a critic of Communism and supported the anti-communist Solidarity movement in Poland. Former Soviet dictator Mikhail Gorbachev once said, "The collapse of the Iron Curtain would have been impossible without John Paul II." When US President George W. Bush presented the Presidential Medal of Freedom to John Paul II, he mentioned how his "principled stand for peace and freedom has inspired millions and helped to topple communism and tyranny."

It was a spiritual, not military, operation. On the one hand, the pope rejected the idea, or ideology, that we are mere individuals, and that society is merely a collection of autonomous, pure egos without any ties or connections—sometimes called the "Crusoe model." On the other hand, he also rejected the opposite idea, or ideology, that individuals only exist for the purpose of society—as is believed in Soviet totalitarianism. There must be something in-between—and that's what Christianity has to offer to the world.

John Paul II would stress repeatedly that human beings are social beings who have human dignity and human rights, independent of society. As early as his first 1979 encyclical, *Redemptor Hominis*, he laid out his agenda for the rest of his papacy. In particular, it set the stage for his confrontation with Communism, rooted in his emphasis on the dignity of the human person. It was like a time bomb. Although the words Marxism and Communism are not found in the encyclical, it is on the idea of the human person that the pope placed the confrontation with Communist collectivism. A few months after the encyclical, John Paul II led a nine-day pilgrimage through Poland, in which one third of the population—thirteen million people—attended at least one of his events. The pilgrimage is credited with fueling the anti-communist Solidarity movement in Poland. It was one of the first dominoes to fall in the eventual collapse of Communism.

In John Paul II's view, society is more than the sum total of its individual members, with all of them having their own positions, responsibilities and relationships within a larger entity. Since human beings have a natural aptitude to live in society with others, they cannot attain their well-being outside of society. When one member is afflicted, all the others are affected. This calls for mutual responsibility and solidarity, instead of laissez-faire individualism, thus opening a middle road focusing on interactions between individuals within the setting of a society. Since humans are fundamentally social beings, rather than individualists, they have a natural tendency to create organizations beyond the individual—which are structures that range from nuclear families, extended families, and clans to cities, states, tribes, organizations, civilizations, cultures and societies.

According to John Paul II, not only are we social beings but also spiritual beings—another insight Communism rejects. Communism represents a militant form of atheism. Aleksandr Solzhenitsyn is very adamant about the way atheistic communism operated in the former Soviet Union during the time he lived there: "Militant atheism is not merely incidental or marginal to Communist policy; it is not a side effect, but the central pivot."

There is something very inconsistent about this form of atheism: it tries to constantly remind us of God while maintaining God does not exist. How could one hate something that is not there? Why would one persistently prove to people the non-existence of a being that is not supposed to exist anyway? Cardinal Stefan Wyszyński, the late Primate of Poland, who dealt most of his life with the aggressive atheism of Soviet Communism, has an astounding answer to these questions: in order to hate God, you must first have faith that there is a God, for only when you firmly believe in God will you be able to hate him. That was the cardinal's explanation for the fact that the Communist media in his country used to persistently mention God in their God-less propaganda against God.

Communism is ultimately rooted in a blatant kind of materialism that has no room for God and religion. We find a social form of materialism in humanism, a collective form of materialism in communism and an individualistic form of materialism in capitalism (not to be confused with a free-market economy). All three share a vision of the human person that is incomplete: it has no longer a spiritual dimension. All three of them deny, or at least ignore, the existence of God.

In contrast, Christianity places God at center stage. It proclaims that each one of us was created in God's image and likeness; and that's where our human dignity and human rights stem from—and no society can take those away, not even Communism. Without that spiritual dimension, human beings become mere material entities—a statistic, at best. Pope Benedict XVI said about John Paul II that he made the world recognize once again "the spiritual dimension of history."

Sadly enough, both dimensions of a human being—social

and spiritual—are foreign to Communism. Not surprisingly, the Church explicitly rejects, in the words of the Catechism (#2425), "the totalitarian and atheistic ideologies associated in modem times with 'communism' or 'socialism.'" They caused enormous destruction in the world. The horrors placed on human beings by totalitarian regimes—in the labor camps run by Nazis, Soviets and Maoists, for instance—tell us how ugly ideologies can get. They turn a society of citizens into a colony of termites, without any social or spiritual dimension. That's what John Paul II worked hard at to avert.

John Paul II is another one of those Catholics who changed the world we live in. He gave the world, curtailed by communism, its social and spiritual dimension back. He tore the iron curtain down.

41

Justin the Martyr: Faith and Reason

There is this very common misconception about religious believers. On weekdays, they are critical, want proofs, look for arguments, and believe something only if there is no further doubt. Then, on Sundays, they turn a switch, set their understanding to zero and their gaze on infinity; they have no need for proofs at all, they open their mouths and swallow revealed truths and absurd dogmas. The contrast painted here is clear: religious believers live a schizophrenic life. It is the life of "reason" on weekdays and the life of "faith" on Sundays.

This portrayal is actually a blatant misconception. Someone who showed us this as early as the second century is one of the first Christian philosophers, Justin the Martyr (100-165).

At an early age, Justin was inspired by the old Greek philosopher Socrates. Socrates had been accused of rejecting pagan idolatry in his search for the one true God. Four centuries later, Justin would be trying to continue, and finally complete, this search for the one true God. Thus, his dialogue with philosophy had begun—at the interface of Christianity and philosophy. Justin began to write philosophy tailored to pagans and Jews. He engaged his pagan adversaries on common ground—philosophy—for he was convinced that a well-developed presentation of Christian Faith would win all thinking persons to Christ. This is what has become known as *apologetics*—an endeavor of trying to present a rational basis for the Christian Faith and to defend it against objections (§0). You may consider philosophy a pretty sophisticated enterprise, but there isn't probably one human being who doesn't philosophize; each one of us is destined to start philosophizing at some point in life. Justin saw that in all clarity.

Justin would wear—for the rest of his life, even as a Christian—the distinctive outfit [*pallium*] of a philosopher. Around 150, he moved to Rome and opened a school of philosophy. As a Christian philosopher, he debated with Roman philosophers, Jewish rabbis and Christian heretics, inviting them to come to the full knowledge of the truth. So what was it then that made him differ as a Christian philosopher from the Greek philosophers? It is, he said, the difference between partial truth and full truth. Justin saw partial truth in pagan philosophy, but considered the *full* truth a legacy of Christian faith. He believed that God himself drew all human beings to himself by planting universal truths in them.

In other words, Justin had become a Christian *apologist*, a defender of the Christian faith—not to be misunderstood as someone who makes an "apology" (far from that). However, we don't remember him only as "Justin the Apologist" but also as "Justin the Martyr." Being an apologist was the reason why he became a martyr. Justin himself had predicted this; Socrates had taught him what is ahead of people who are in search of truth in a pagan society: "I too, therefore, expect to be plotted against and fixed to the stake." This is indeed what happened when Marcus Aurelius, a philosopher like Justin, became emperor in 161. He too would always wear his distinctive

41 Justin the Martyr: Faith and Reason

"pallium." However, one of his first official acts as emperor was to usher in a new round of persecution—the fourth one in early Church's history. And the most famous victim would be Justin himself.

Was Justin's ministry a new invention? Not really. In fact, Justin had taken on the ministry pioneered already by the Apostle Paul (§52), who around 51 went to Athens where he still saw idols everywhere, but also an opening for Christianity: "For as I walked around looking carefully at your shrines, I even discovered an altar inscribed, 'To an Unknown God.' What therefore you unknowingly worship, I proclaim to you." Paul went as far as quoting some of their own poets in his speech on the Areopagus in Athens: "For 'In him we live and move and have our being,' as even some of your poets have said, 'For we too are his offspring'" (Acts 17:28).

So what Justin tried to do was certainly not new in Christianity. Call Justin's approach whatever you want—a vision, a conviction, a motto, a principle, an idea—it is ultimately a core truth that has been a driving force in the history of the Catholic Church. It has taken on various expressions, but the idea behind it always remained the same: an encounter between religion and philosophy, between faith and reason, and later between religion and science. They are not each other's foes, but each other's allies (§1). There is no conflict between them, but only harmony.

What Justin had started and proclaimed was later translated in various other ways. We find it back, for instance, in Augustine's two famous formulas from around the year 400, "Believe in order to understand" [*Crede ut intelligas*], but also, and inseparably, "Understand in order to believe" [*intellige ut credas*]. In other words, in order to find God and believe, you must scrutinize faith *as well as* reason. Augustine could not have translated Justin's insight more clearly, "Believers are also thinkers: in believing, they think and in thinking, they believe."

We find this same theme back also in Anselm's two famous phrases from the 11th century, "Faith seeking understanding" and "I believe in order that I might understand." Anselm is more or less saying that faith helps you understand everything better, but also that faith has to be understood by reason so it doesn't become irrational.

This Catholic understanding of faith became even more pronounced when Thomas Aquinas (§60) came along. Aquinas argued against the idea of some people that when we begin to use reason, we have no choice but to abandon faith, or conversely, that if we have faith, we must leave reason behind. Aquinas declared the opposite: What we know through reason can never be in conflict with what we know through faith, and what we know through faith can never be in violation of what we know through reasoning.

This has become known as the Catholic conception of *Faith and Reason*: we should be faithful in our reasoning and reasonable in our faith—even when, or specifically when, it comes to God. We cannot live by faith alone neither by reason alone, but only by a harmonious combination of faith *and* reason. Sometimes we need understanding before we can believe, at other times we need faith before we can understand. Faith tells us more than we could know by reason alone, so we need to become "faithful" in our reasoning. On the other hand, reason tells us more than we could know by faith alone, so we need to become "reasonable" in our faith.

The Catholic Church will always be known for her motto "Faith *and* Reason." She is arguably unique in Christianity, and even among other religions, in so strongly advancing the role of reason in religion. In many religions, you can find beliefs that

41 Justin the Martyr: Faith and Reason

make no sense at all. In contrast, the Catholic Church does not accept beliefs that go against reason or are otherwise unreasonable. In this, she follows a long history that began with Justin, or actually with the Apostle Paul. Catholicism is arguably the most rational and coherent of all religions. When it comes to faith, Catholics are encouraged to use their heads. They don't believe that religious faith is immune to rational argumentation and to scrutiny by reason. Catholics are thinkers: in believing they think, and in thinking they believe.

Pope John Paul II reinforced what Justin had started. In his encyclical "Faith *and* Reason" [*Fides et Ratio*], he referred to Justin the Martyr who used philosophy as a preparation to the Faith. He also explained, "Faith and reason are like two wings on which the human spirit rises to the contemplation of truth; and God has placed in the human heart a desire to know the truth—in a word, to know himself—so that, by knowing and loving God, men and women may also come to the fullness of truth about themselves." Faith and reason combined form the cradle of truth. Therefore, we need to reject both a faith-alone approach and a reason-alone approach.

When the father of a college student heard his daughter was learning that theology was "faith seeking understanding," he exclaimed: "But faith doesn't have to seek understanding—that's why they call it faith!" Such people seem to reason (!) that if God's existence were a matter of proof, it would no longer be a matter of faith—therefore, it cannot be a matter of proof either. Some Christians trace this idea back to the German Reformer Martin Luther, who once said, "Reason is the greatest enemy that faith has." Justin would have told him differently. In faith, you cannot believe something that is completely irrational or incomprehensible.

Justin the Martyr is another one of those Catholics who

changed the world we live in. He showed the world that Catholics are thinkers: in believing they think, and in thinking they believe.

42

Landsteiner, Karl: Blood Transfusions

There is something magical about blood. For centuries, people used to think that differences in temperament, talents, social status, wealth and power had to reside "in the blood." They used to speak in terms of "blood" ties; terms such as "blood relative," "bloodline," "full-blooded," and "royal blood" are relics of this idea. Now we know that's not the case, but blood remains a "vital" component of our body.

We are so used to blood transfusions that we might easily think that's the way the world has always been. Indeed, "bloodletting"—also called phlebotomy—is probably as old as humanity. Early "phlebotomists" used techniques such as leeches and incisions to extract blood from the body in order to remove toxins from the body. But blood transfusion is a different story.

The first recorded successful blood transfusion occurred in England in 1665, when Richard Lower kept dogs alive by transfusing blood from one dog to another dog. In 1818, James Blundell performed the first successful transfusion of human blood to a patient for the treatment of postpartum hemorrhage. That may sound encouraging, but soon it was found out that many patients could die from blood transfusions. Often, what was supposed to save people's life made them in fact lose it. By the late 19th century, blood transfusion was regarded as a risky and dubious procedure, and it was largely shunned by the medical establishment.

Although technically possible, blood transfusion failed too often. Why? The person who would finally answer this question was Karl Landsteiner (1868-1943).

Karl Landsteiner's parents were Jews, but in December 1890, Karl and his then widowed mother converted to Catholicism. At age 22, Karl was baptized with the name Karl Otto. Two months later, Landsteiner received his degree in medicine. In 1916, he married Leopoldine Helene Wlasto, a Greek Orthodox who converted to her husband's Catholic faith.

In the meantime, Landsteiner was on his way to becoming quite famous. In 1900, he found that mixing blood from two "incompatible" individuals has adverse, even fatal effects because an immune response is triggered making the red blood cells clump. He had in fact discovered the now well-known ABO blood group system, based on four blood types—A, B, AB and O. Through this discovery, he had found a way for blood transfusions to be carried out much more safely and successfully. For this discovery he was awarded the Nobel Prize in Physiology or Medicine in 1930.

Then, in 1939, he discovered another blood group system, the Rhesus system, which can also cause fatal results, especially around pregnancy. Thanks to Landsteiner's discovery, such effects can be prevented. In addition to the ABO system and the Rhesus system, we have learned there are in fact thirty-two different blood group systems. Since most blood group systems show very little variability within a specific population, blood transfusion complications have been very rare, except for the ABO and Rhesus systems. Most of the other thirty systems were discovered after Landsteiner's death in 1943, but he had made them possible.

Though he was praised for his discoveries, Landsteiner's life had not become easier. After World War I, Vienna and the new republic of Austria as a whole were in a desolate economic state, a situation in which Landsteiner did not see any possibilities to carry on with his research work. He decided to move to The Netherlands and accepted a small post at the Catholic St. Johannes de Deo hospital in The Hague. He also authored a number of papers, five of them to be published in Dutch by the Royal Academy of Sciences.

Yet working conditions in The Hague proved to be not much better than in post-war Vienna. So Landsteiner accepted an invitation from New York, initiated by Simon Flexner, who was familiar with Landsteiner's achievements, to work for the Rockefeller Institute. He arrived In New York with his family in the spring of 1923. Throughout the 1920s, Landsteiner worked there on problems related to immunity and allergy. In 1927, he discovered, with Levine and Wiener, two new blood group systems: the P system, and the M and N system, refining the work he had begun 20 years earlier.

Karl Landsteiner is another one of those Catholics who changed the world we live in. He saved many lives by making blood transfusion a routine medical practice.

43

Lemaître, Georges: Big Bang

All the evidence available today seems to indicate that the Universe has not existed forever, but did have a beginning, called the Big Bang, about 14 billion years ago. That in itself is quite amazing, for there is no logical contradiction in the notion of a Universe without a beginning. It could be possible, for instance, that explosions and collapses follow each other in an endless sequence of expanding and contracting. If that were the case, then the Universe might have never had a beginning. Aristotle, for one, did not believe in a beginning of the Universe, nor did most scientists in the early 20th century.

But things changed dramatically when the Big Bang theory was launched. Until then, most scientists believed in a static universe that has no beginning and no end. We know, for instance, that even Albert Einstein held on to a steady-state model of the universe. But all of a sudden the universe was given a beginning! The person who launched the idea that the Big Bang was the beginning of the universe was George Lemaître (1894-1966).

George Lemaître was a Belgian Catholic Priest, astronomer and professor of physics at the Catholic University of Leuven. Born in Charleroi, Belgium, he studied at a Jesuit secondary

43 Lemaître, Georges: Big Bang

school, the Collège du Sacré-Coeur, in Charleroi, and then began studying civil engineering at the Catholic University of Leuven at the age of 17. In 1914, he interrupted his studies to serve as an artillery officer in the Belgian army for the duration of World War I. After the war, he studied physics and mathematics, and began to prepare for the diocesan priesthood. In 1923, he became a graduate student in astronomy at the University of Cambridge, England, and soon after, at MIT in Cambridge, Massachusetts. In 1925, on his return to Belgium, he started teaching at the Catholic University of Leuven, Belgium.

Lemaître was the first man to propose the concept of an expanding universe. In 1929, Edwin Hubble had discovered that all very distant galaxies have an apparent velocity directly away from us: the farther away, the higher their apparent velocity—an idea which had already been suggested in 1927 by Lemaître himself. In 1931, Lemaître went even further and suggested that the evident expansion of the Universe, if projected back in time, meant that the farther back into the past the smaller the Universe was, until at some finite time in the past, all the mass of the Universe was concentrated in a single point—a "primeval atom," in Lemaître's own words. That's where and when the fabric of time and space must have started. Time and space are like the "fabric" or "matrix" of the Universe.

Lemaître's hypothesis would soon be called the "Big Bang" theory, a term coined by the English astronomer Fred Hoyle during a 1949 radio broadcast. Currently, the Big Bang theory is the prevailing cosmological model that explains the early development of the Universe. According to this theory, the Universe was once in an extremely hot and dense state which then expanded rapidly. This rapid expansion caused the Universe to cool and resulted in its present continuously expanding state. Once it had cooled sufficiently, its energy was allowed to be converted into various subatomic particles, including protons, neutrons, and electrons. Giant clouds of these primordial elements would then coalesce through gravity to form stars and galaxies, and the heavier elements would be synthesized either within stars or during supernovae. Interestingly enough, the 92 elements we find on earth can be found all over the Universe, indicating a common origin.

Ironically, Albert Einstein was very hesitant to accept the idea that the Universe was created during a single explosive event. He never in his lifetime accepted the Big Bang as the way our universe came into being, and always looked for another explanation. Instead, he believed that the universe expanded steadily and eternally. After he had studied Lemaître's 1927 paper intensely, Einstein told the priest, "Your mathematics is perfect, but your physics is abominable." Einstein would one day take back those words, though, but his valid point was that mathematics does not have the last word in physics.

It is thanks to the Big Bang Theory that we can now raise the question of the beginning of time. As strange as it may sound, time is something that *began* at "one point in time." Albert Einstein had already showed us that both time and space are part of the physical world, just as much as matter and energy. Since space-time is something that not always existed, one might think there must have been a "time" when there was no time and space—which cannot literally be true, of course.

A beginning of time, really? Yes, the Catholic Church had already proclaimed this in 1215, when the Fourth Lateran Council taught that the universe was created "out of nothing at the beginning of time"—an idea which would have scandalized most ancient Greeks as well as most nineteenth-century scientists, but which is now a commonplace of modern cosmology.

It is amazing how the Church, without any scientific input, knew already long ago that the world not only has an ending but also a beginning. In other words, God did not create the world in time, but with time—or having time in it. God did not create the world in space, but he created space in the world—or a world full of space. From out of his very Being, God gives being to the whole world and all things in it, including time and space.

Obviously the *creation* of the universe cannot be studied by the natural sciences, and should not be confused with the Big Bang. The Big Bang is not the creation of the universe. Let's keep our terminology straight. Thomas Aquinas (§60) makes an important distinction between producing [*facere*] and creating [*creare*]. Science is about "producing" something from something else—it is about changes taking place in this Universe. Creation, on the other hand, is about "creating" something from nothing—which is not a change at all; certainly not a change from "nothing" to "something." In other words, God the Creator doesn't just take pre-existing stuff and fashion it, as does the Demiurge in Plato's *Timaeus*. Nor does the Creator use some something called "nothing" and then create the Universe out of that. Rather, God calls the Universe into existence without using pre-existing space, matter, time, or anything else. That's what "creation" means.

Therefore, *creating* something "out of nothing" is not *producing* something out of nothing—that would be a conceptual mistake, for it erroneously treats "nothing" as some kind of something. In contrast, the Christian doctrine of creation "out of nothing" [*ex nihilo*] claims that God made the Universe without making it out of anything. Creation has everything to do with the philosophical and theological question as to why things exist at all, before they can even undergo change. Consequently, creation—but certainly not the Big Bang—is the reason why there is something rather than nothing. Science is about "producing" something from *something* else; religion is about "creating" something from *nothing*.

In other words, God *creates* something whereas the Big Bang *produces* something. Creation does not mean changing a no-thing into a some-thing, or changing something into something else—similar to the way chemists change water into hydrogen and oxygen. Creation means bringing everything into being and existence. Obviously, the unfolding of the Universe, starting with the Big Bang, is a process that plays in time and can be studied by the physical sciences. Creation, on the other hand, cannot follow a timeline, as time itself is a product of creation as well. Even Augustine knew this long ago, "There can be no time without creation."

In this specific sense, creation must come "first" before any events, even a Big Bang, can follow. However, creation in itself is not an event at all, so it cannot literally come "first" in time. Creation concerns the *origin* of the Universe—its source of being—not its *beginning* in time. So creation must come "first" in the order of primacy, not in the order of time. Creation is not something that happened long ago in time, and neither is the Creator someone who did something in the distant past because the Creator does something "at all times"—by keeping a contingent world in existence, continually and faithfully. If rightly understood, creation is not a "one-time deal," but it copes instead with the question as to where this Universe ultimately comes from, as to how it came into being and how it stays in existence. The answer is that it does not come from the Big Bang, but may have started with the Big Bang.

George Lemaître spoke about the God of the Big Bang as the

"One Who gave us the mind to understand him and to recognize a glimpse of his glory in our Universe which he has so wonderfully adjusted to the mental power with which he has endowed us."

George Lemaître is another one of those Catholics who changed the world we live in—not the world itself, of course, but the way we look at the world. He made our world part of an enormous, expanding Universe, which shows the grandeur of the Creator.

44

Leo XIII: Social Teaching

It is a constant challenge for the Catholic Church to deal with a changing world while keeping the core of her message and doctrines unchanged. How does the Church adjust to what is new without losing what's old? She can't reject the continuity of her tradition nor can she reject the change that's taking place around her. That creates a tense dilemma.

The Church has actually faced such dilemmas repeatedly. With the rise of fascism and Nazism, the Church had to develop her teaching on the dignity of all human beings (§54). And in the wake of the sexual revolution and breakdown of the family in the 20th century, the Church has had to re-emphasize the importance of marriage and family life (§53).

Another occasion like these was created by the rise of Marxism, socialism and capitalism in the 19th century. The key player in this confrontation was Pope Leo XIII (1810-1903).

Leo XIII was born in Carpineto Romano, near Rome, with the name of Vincenzo Pecci. He was the sixth of the seven sons of Count Ludovico Pecci and his wife Anna Prosperi Buzzi. In 1824, Vincenzo and his older brother Giuseppe were called to Rome where their mother was dying. Count Pecci wanted his children near him after the loss of his wife, and so they stayed with him in Rome, attending the Jesuit Roman College. There Vincenzo had a chance to shine.

As soon as he was elected to the papacy, Leo XIII worked to encourage understanding between the Church and the modern world. More in particular, he tried to reconcile the Church with the working class, specifically by dealing with the social and economic changes that were sweeping Europe. The new economic order had resulted in the growth of an impoverished working class which had increasing anti-clerical and socialist sympathies. Leo helped reverse this trend.

It was very clear to him that the Industrial Revolution had changed the world. The old system of *guilds*—the socio-economic backbone of the past—was crumbling. Founded in the Middle Ages, the guilds had been social, economic and religious all at once. Guildsmen trained the young in their trades; they maintained a high standard of quality; they provided stability in costs and profit; they cared for their invalid members and their widows and orphans; and they came together in the worship of God, especially to celebrate their patronal feasts. The abolition of the guilds, then, left a void between worker and master.

Leo saw very clearly that the Industrial Revolution had opened the gate for two new ideologies: socialism and capitalism, with socialism exclusively focusing on the worker, and capitalism on the master. He described the ensuing situation very aptly in one of his encyclicals: "For the result of civil change and revolution has been to divide cities into two classes separated by a wide chasm. On the one side there is the party which holds power because it holds wealth.... On the other side there is the needy and powerless multitude, sick and sore in spirit and ever ready for disturbance." The pontiff also saw very clearly that neither socialism nor capitalism were the answer to the problem. In his encyclicals, he argued very convincingly that both capitalism and communism are flawed.

What is wrong with *capitalism* in Leo's eyes? He didn't believe in an economic system that puts profits before people—sometimes called "laissez-faire" capitalism. In his encyclicals, he would call out greedy industrialists for abusing workers. He was seriously concerned with capitalism's disruptive social effects. Long before the world gave much thought to the needs of common laborers and their families, Leo defended the rights of the worker against capitalism. While he does not present industrial capitalism as something to be opposed entirely, he rigorously affirms private property—without absolutizing it, though—and insists that there are natural inequalities between people willed by God which are necessary for society to flourish.

What is wrong with *socialism* in Leo's eyes? When he speaks of socialism he also includes communism, and reversed. Socialism and communism both promote an economic system that seeks to achieve extreme equality among members of society. Communism adds to this a political ideology that rejects religion, advocates a classless and stateless society, and declares all property and possessions common property, to be administered by the State (§40). Communism is regarded as a more extreme form of socialism. What unites them, though, is that both downright oppose capitalism.

Leo's second encyclical of 1878, *Quod Apostolici Muneris*, dealt directly with the topic of socialism. Not mincing words, Leo bluntly stated that socialism—in whatever form—corrupts the state, damages the family, violates legitimate property rights, contradicts the commandment against theft, and, above all, is contrary to divine and natural law (§46). Nearly one-third of his famous 1891 encyclical *Rerum novarum* [On New Things] is devoted to proving that socialism does not possess the answer to the social crisis, since it would do as much harm to the workers as it might help them. He explained again the sad deficiencies of socialism—its atheistic materialism, its doctrine and practice of class-war, its denial of the rights and liberties of the human person, including the natural right to possess some measure of private property, and its contempt for good morals—and he gave an early warning of the misery it would inflict on the world. His words were prophetic.

So now the question is: how could Leo navigate between the Scylla of capitalism and Charybdis of socialism? Especially in his 1891 encyclical, *Rerum novarum*, Leo set out the Catholic Church's response to the social instability and labor conflict that had arisen in the wake of industrialization and had led to the rise of socialism and capitalism. He advocated that it's the role of the State to promote social justice through the protection of rights, while the Church must speak out on social issues in order to teach correct social principles and ensure class harmony. More specifically, his encyclical discussed various contentious social issues:

- Regarding the role of the classes, the pope calls for cooperation among the classes—not class warfare.
- Regarding the role of the state, Leo defends the basic rights of the individual and the family and their priority with regard to the state. Therefore, he warns against excessive state economic intervention, especially against efforts to replace the Church's charitable and anti-poverty work with government agencies.
- Regarding the role of the family, Leo sees the family as, in his own words, "a society very small, one must admit, but none the less a true society, and one older than any state." He noted that socialism, more in particular

communism, destroys families: "The contention, then, that the civil government should at its option intrude into and exercise intimate control over the family and the household, is a great and pernicious error."

-Regarding the role of private property, Leo insists, "The first and most fundamental principle, therefore, if one would undertake to alleviate the condition of the masses, must be the inviolability of private property." He sought a Christian basis for property rights in the fact that man is created in the image of God.

-Regarding the role of the worker—perhaps the most controversial issue—Leo outlined the rights of workers to a fair wage, safe working conditions, and the formation of labor unions (§55). Not surprisingly, he has been called "the Pope of the Worker."

All in all, at a time of great social upheaval, the encyclical sketched out a uniquely Catholic response to the challenges of worker rights, urbanization, industrialization—avoiding the extremes of both socialism and laissez-faire capitalism. As G.K. Chesterton (§17) would say later on, "It is vain to criticize socialism without confessing the colossal blunder of capitalism." Leo realized very well that, in his own words, "capital needs labor and labor needs capital."

Rerum novarum also introduced into Catholic social thought the concept of *subsidiarity*, the principle that political and social decisions should be taken at a local level, if possible, rather than by a central authority. With this principle, Leo made an attempt to articulate again a middle course between laissez-faire capitalism and the communist form of socialism, which subordinates the individual to the State. Subsidiarity locates the responsibilities and privileges of social life in the smallest unit of organization at which they will function. Larger social bodies, be they the State or otherwise, are permitted and required to intervene only when smaller ones cannot carry out the tasks themselves (§48).

It is no exaggeration to say that Pope Leo XIII is the father of modern Catholic social teaching. Pope John XXIII called *Rerum Novarum* the magna carta of Catholic social teaching. As Pope John Paul II recognized 100 years after its initial promulgation, it provided a key first step for the Church in addressing the dominant social question of the time: the exploitation and suffering of workers that was the byproduct of the Industrial Revolution.

Pope Leo XIII is another one of those Catholics who changed the world we live in. Western civilization owes much to him for its stand on the social question.

45

Lewis, C.S.: Apologetics

With regards to religion, the word "faith" is probably one of the most abused words in modern terminology. Its meaning ranges from "blind faith" to "proven faith," from "a leap of faith" to "the security of faith," from "fiction" to "nonfiction," from "wishful thinking" to "fact-based thinking," from "belief" to "knowledge," from a "feeling" to a "doctrine," from a "childish delusion" to a "grown-up realism," from "opinions" to "truths," from "irrational beliefs" to "factual propositions," from "unfounded ideas" to "rational conclusions." All of these are extremes, of course.

Apologetics may help us to navigate between these extremes. Apologetics is an endeavor of trying to present a rational basis for the Christian faith and to defend it against objections and misrepresentations. It defends the truth of religious doctrines through systematic argumentation and discourse. It does so by the use of *reason* to explain the truths of faith and to defend the truths of faith (§41). Faith is based on a series of supernatural truths—truths such as that there is a God, that God is the maker of heaven and earth, that Jesus is the Son of God, that Jesus redeemed us from sin, etc. Although these truths cannot be *proven* with rational arguments, they

45 Lewis, C. S.: Apologetics

can be *defended* with rational arguments. That's what apologetics tries to do.

There was this car salesman who had been talking successfully with one of his clients. When he thought the deal was ready to be made, the client suddenly took off. The salesman went to his boss and told him, "Sorry, Sir, I had taken the client to the water but I could not make him drink." In response, the boss told him, "It's not your task to make people drink but to make them thirsty."

That's basically what apologetics is supposed to do: not forcing people to "drink," but making people "thirsty." It does not end up at either end of the extremes mentioned at the beginning. It does not prove the faith beyond any doubt but makes it reasonable, acceptable and ultimately attractive. The person who was a master in doing this was C.S. Lewis (1898-1966).

C.S. Lewis was born in Belfast, Ireland, as Clive Staples Lewis—more commonly abbreviated to C.S. Lewis. His father was Albert James Lewis, a solicitor whose father, Richard Lewis, had come to Ireland from Wales during the mid-19th century. His mother was Florence Augusta Lewis (née Hamilton), known as Flora, the daughter of a Church of Ireland priest, and great grand-daughter of both Bishop Hugh Hamilton and John Staples. So he was raised in a religious family that attended the Protestant Church of Ireland.

Lewis became an atheist at age 15, which he later described paradoxically as, "I maintained that God did not exist. I was also very angry with God for not existing." In 1916, at age 18, Lewis was awarded a scholarship at University College, Oxford. Within months of entering Oxford, the British Army shipped him to France to fight in the First World War. His experience of the horror of war only confirmed his atheism.

After Lewis returned to Oxford University, he became a philosophy tutor at University College and, in 1925, was elected a Fellow and Tutor in English Literature at Magdalen College in Cambridge, where he served for 29 years until 1954. In 1954, Lewis accepted the newly founded chair of Mediaeval and Renaissance Literature at Magdalene College, where he finished his career. He maintained a strong attachment to the city of Oxford, keeping a home there and returning on weekends until his death in 1963.

During his academic career, Lewis returned to Anglicanism at the age of 32, although he vigorously resisted conversion, noting that he was brought into Christianity like a prodigal, "kicking, struggling, resentful, and darting his eyes in every direction for a chance to escape." But he could not escape the arguments he had with the Catholic novelist J. R. R. Tolkien—the famous author of *Lords of the Ring*—whom he seems to have met for the first time in 1926. Lewis and Tolkien became close friends. They both served on the English faculty at Oxford University, and were active in the informal Oxford literary group known as the Inklings. Lewis was also much influenced by the book *The Everlasting Man* written by G. K. Chesterton (§17).

Owing to the influence of Tolkien, Chesterton and some other friends, Lewis became a member of the Church of England—somewhat to the disappointment of Tolkien, who had hoped that he would join the Catholic Church. Yet, Lewis had decided, as he put it in his own words, to become an "ordinary layman of the Church of England." From then on, he considered himself an entirely orthodox Anglican to the end of his life, very interested in presenting a reasonable case for Christianity. Lewis was a committed Anglican who upheld a largely orthodox Anglican theology, though in his apologetic

45 Lewis, C. S.: Apologetics

writings, he made an effort to avoid espousing any one denomination.

Lewis's faith profoundly affected his work, and his wartime radio broadcasts on the subject of Christianity brought him wide acclaim. His books *Mere Christianity*, *The Problem of Pain*, and *Miracles* were all concerned, to one degree or another, with refuting popular objections to Christianity, such as the question, "How could a good God allow pain to exist in the world?" *Mere Christianity* was voted best book of the twentieth century by *Christianity Today* in 2000.

Here are a few nuggets of his apologetics:

- About Jesus, "Either this man was, and is, the Son of God, or else a madman or something worse."
- Lewis called Hell, "the greatest monument to human freedom."
- "If there was a controlling power outside the Universe, it could not show itself to us as one of the facts inside the Universe—no more than the architect of a house could actually be a wall or staircase or fireplace in that house."
- "The human mind has no more power of inventing a new [moral] value than of imagining a new primary color."
- "I believe in Christianity as I believe that the sun has risen: not only because I see it, but because by it I see everything else."
- "[I]f there were no light in the Universe and therefore no creatures with eyes, we would never know it was dark."
- "[Those] who did most for the present world were just those who thought most of the next."
- "There are only two kinds of people—those who say to God, 'Thy will be done' and those to whom God says in the end, 'Thy will be done.'"

You may wonder by now whether Lewis, not being a Catholic himself, belongs in this book about Catholics. Although the reading of Catholic authors such as Chesterton, and the friendship with Catholics such as Tolkien, played a crucial role in Lewis' conversion from atheism to Christianity, he was never seriously tempted to cross the Tiber into the Catholic Church. And yet, in spite of the residual anti-papist prejudice that he had inherited as a Belfast Protestant, many of the core beliefs he embraced as a "mere Christian" placed him decidedly on the Catholic end of the theological spectrum. He believed in the real presence of Christ in the Eucharist, which he referred to as the Blessed Sacrament; he practiced auricular confession; he vehemently opposed female ordination, condemning in forthright terms the danger of having "priestesses in the Church"; he declared his belief in purgatory and in the efficacy of praying for the dead; and, last but not least, he crusaded against the errors and heresies of theological modernism.

It is, therefore, perhaps not so surprising that C.S. Lewis has ushered so many people into the Catholic Church. A powerful part of C.S. Lewis' legacy is the impact he has had on the conversion of countless numbers of people to the Catholic Church. The great American literary convert Walker Percy, commenting on the numerous converts who had come to Catholicism through the writings of Lewis, remarked that "writers one might expect, from Aquinas to Merton," are mentioned frequently as influences, "but guess who turns up most often? C.S. Lewis!—who, if he didn't make it all the way, certainly handed over a goodly crew."

Here are just two of them. Catholic philosopher Peter Kreeft believes *Mere Christianity* "has probably accounted for more conversions than any other book in the century." And Ross

Douthat, a Catholic *New York Times* columnist, summarized C.S. Lewis' role as follows: "You start reading C.S. Lewis, then you're reading G.K. Chesterton, then you're a Catholic. I knew a lot of people who did that in their 20s—I just did it earlier."

    C.S. Lewis is another one of those "Catholics" who changed the world we live in. He may not have made people "drink," but he certainly made thousands of people "thirsty" for Christianity, even for Catholicism.

46

Maritain, Jacques: Human Rights

Not a day goes by that we hear something in the news about human rights. I am sure those rights did not come out of the blue, so you wonder where the idea of human rights did come from then.

If this were a question in a quiz, probably many would answer that human-rights talk originated in 1948 in the United Nations (UN). That's indeed the year when the UN affirmed in its *Universal Declaration of Human Rights* that "all human beings are born free and equal in dignity and rights." The UN Declaration also declared that human rights flow from "the inherent dignity of the human person."

But then you might ask yourself the next question: where did such deep insights as expressed in the UN Declaration actually come from? Scholars would say that they had a long history. Documents asserting individual rights, such as the Magna Carta (1215), the Petition of Right (1628), the US Constitution (1787), the French Declaration of the Rights of Man and of the Citizen (1789), and the US Bill of Rights (1791) are the written precursors to many of today's human rights documents. But let's skip that issue here and focus more explicitly on who in particular promoted the idea of human rights in the United Nations.

In 1946, the United Nations Educational, Scientific, and Cultural Organization (UNESCO) had appointed a committee composed of many of the leading thinkers of the day to search for areas of potential agreement among different cultural and philosophical traditions. This committee had the prominent Catholic philosopher Jacques Maritain as one of its most active members. Who was Jacques Maritain (1882-1973)?

Jacques Maritain was born in Paris, the son of Paul Maritain, who was a lawyer, and his wife Geneviève Favre. He was reared in a liberal Protestant environment. He was sent to the Lycée Henri-IV. Later, he attended the Sorbonne, studying the natural sciences: chemistry, biology and physics. At the Sorbonne, he met Raïssa Oumançoff, a Russian Jewish émigré. After their marriage in 1904, the young couple started to read, and met their unlikely spiritual godfather, the Catholic convert and novelist Leon Bloy. Thus started the tale of the Maritain's conversion. By 1905, under Bloy's influence, their over-riding life's purpose was "to become holy even as their heavenly father was holy, to become saints."

With Raïssa taking the lead, they started to divide their days up around spiritual exercises. Under Bloy's influence, they became especially attached to Our Lady of LaSalette. Then, by the mid-1920s and 1930s, Maritain had started to immerse himself in the study of Thomas Aquinas (§60). Becoming the author of more than 60 books, he helped revive Aquinas for modern times. It was in this qualification as a Thomist philosopher that Maritain helped form the basis for international law and human rights law in his numerous writings.

Given his background, Maritain was a perfect fit for the UNESCO committee on human rights. During his tenure as

France's envoy to the Holy See between 1945 and 1948, Maritain would also be active to draft the Universal Declaration of Human Rights. This was not an easy task, for the members of the committee had lots of agreements and disagreements.

On the one hand, there was the common understanding of "human rights" as inalienable, fundamental rights to which a person is inherently entitled simply because he or she is a human being. These rights are inherent in all human beings regardless of their nation, location, language, religion, ethnic origin, or any other status. In other words, they are applicable everywhere and at every time in the sense of being universal, and they are egalitarian in the sense of being the same for everyone (§8).

On the other hand, while there was consensus that human rights encompass a wide variety of rights—such as the right to a fair trial, protection against enslavement, prohibition of genocide, free speech or a right to education—there was disagreement about which of these specific rights should be included within the general framework of human rights. However, the fact that an agreement could be achieved across cultures on several practical concepts was "enough," Maritain wrote, "to enable a great task to be undertaken." Maritain was just happy that Christians and non-Christians could find at least a bare minimum of moral agreement. "No declaration of human rights will ever be exhaustive or final," Maritain concluded after pondering the history of rights ideas.

But one key question remained unsettled. The drafters famously left the term "right" vague in order to achieve passage, so it became a placeholder for whatever anyone wants to add later, such as gay rights and even animal rights. Maritain expressed this, rather paradoxically yet very clearly, "We agree on these rights, on condition that no one asks us why." The UN left that question unanswered, and could probably never have given an answer on behalf of all parties involved.

But we cannot really leave that question unanswered: Why should we even talk about human rights? What is their ultimate foundation? If such questions cannot be posed, the whole idea of human rights would be resting on quicksand. If we don't know where human rights come from, how can we ever agree then on which human rights qualify to be on the list? No wonder, that issue had intentionally been left vague in the UN *Declaration of Human Rights*.

If human rights were simply a creation of the human intellect, then it is very difficult to argue that they are universal and that all governments are obligated to honor rights they might even disagree with. Of central importance is Maritain's argument that natural rights are rooted in the *natural law*—a concept also going back to his mentor Thomas Aquinas. As a strong defender of a natural law ethics, Maritain viewed ethical norms as being rooted in human nature. For Maritain, we know the natural law through our direct acquaintance with it in our human experience.

So the prevailing question is: Where does the natural law come from? The natural law is etched in our nature and our hearts by the Creator who made us in his likeness and endowed us with human freedom and human dignity. As the theologian Fr. Mark A. Pilon puts it, "Western nations today have lost any valid understanding of natural rights because it has undercut the rational grounds for these rights. Rational grounds ultimately require a lawmaker, far above the limitations of human positive law." This means that there are no moral rights and no moral duties without God. An absolute law can only come from and be enforced by an absolute Authority. Interestingly enough, even an atheist such as the French philosopher Jean-Paul Sartre realized that there can be no absolute and objective standards of right and wrong if there is no eternal Heaven that would make moral laws and values objective and universal.

The German philosopher Friedrich Nietzsche was another atheist to realize how devastating the decline of religion has been to the morality of society, when he wrote, "God is dead; but as the human race is constituted, there will perhaps be caves for millenniums yet, in which people will show his shadow." Nietzsche is saying here that humanism and other "moral" ideologies shelter themselves in caves and venerate shadows of the God they once believed in; now they are holding on to something they cannot provide themselves, mere shadows of the past. They are merely "idols" constructed to preserve the essence of morality without the substance. As Nietzsche put it, we can still venerate "idols from the past." That's basically what the UN *Declaration of Human Rights* had to do, too.

Therefore, we must come to the conclusion that human rights and human dignity, which are intricately connected, come from "Above"—there is no other way to validate them. Moral laws, moral values, moral rights and moral duties ultimately reside in Heaven. They are real because they come with Creation. We ought to do what we ought to do—for Heaven's sake! The 1776 *United States Declaration of Independence* declared—much more explicitly than the 1948 *Universal Declaration of Human Rights* did—that we are endowed by our Creator with certain "unalienable rights." In other words, human rights are not man-made, but God-given. The only reason we have human rights is that God endows us with rights.

Therefore, "equality in dignity and rights" would be sitting on quicksand, subject to the mercy of law makers and majority votes, if it had no firm foundation in Heaven. It is through the voice of God in the natural law that we know about right and wrong, about human rights and human duties. Without God, who is the author of human rights, we would have no "right" to claim any rights. If there were no God, we could not defend any of those rights we think we have the "right" to defend. We would only have (legal) *entitlements*, which the government provides, but no (moral) *rights*, which God alone can provide. The late President John F. Kennedy put it well in his Inaugural Address: "[T]he rights of man come not from the generosity of the state, but from the hand of God." If these rights did not come from God, people could take them away at any time—which they certainly have tried to do numerous times.

Jacques Maritain is another one of those Catholics who changed the world we live in. He showed us that a world without God-given human rights and human dignity is in serious danger.

47

McCorvey, Norma: Abortion

The practice of abortion—the medical removal of an unborn baby from a woman's womb on her request—has always been a conflict of interests: the interests of the mother versus the interests of the child. It is a conflict that has been known since at least ancient times. In the interest of the mother, various methods were used to perform an abortion, including the administration of abortifacient herbs, the use of sharpened implements, the application of abdominal pressure and other techniques. In the interest of the child, such techniques had to be outlawed; therefore, the Hippocratic Oath explicitly forbade the use of medical techniques to induce abortion, no matter what the woman's interests were.

But times have changed. Especially since the so-called Sexual Revolution (§53), the "demand" for abortion has been skyrocketing, causing many women to claim they should be granted the "right" to obtain an abortion. In the USA, for instance, the process of legalizing abortion was propelled by two people in particular. One was Dr. Bernard Nathanson (1926-2011), the OB-GYN from New York City, who became the director of New York's Center for Reproductive and Sexual Health, the largest freestanding abortion facility in the world.

47 McCorvey, Norma: Abortion

The other person in the fight for abortion was Norma McCorvey (1947-2017). When local attorneys and activists in Dallas, TX, were ready to challenge the State's anti-abortion law, they took as their case an unmarried, unemployed young woman, who was denied access to abortion when she became pregnant. That person was Norma McCorvey, who went by a different name in the case: Jane Roe, or the "Roe" in *Roe v. Wade*.

In 1970, Norma McCorvey, under the pseudonym "Jane Roe," filed a law suit challenging the Texas laws that criminalized abortion. She is described as a pregnant woman who "wished to terminate her pregnancy by an abortion 'performed by a competent, licensed physician, under safe, clinical conditions'; that she was unable to get a 'legal' abortion in Texas.... She claimed that the Texas statutes were unconstitutionally vague and that they abridged her right of personal privacy" (Roe v. Wade, 410 U.S. 113 (1973), 120).

Eventually, the case reached the U.S. Supreme Court in 1973 thus becoming the now-famous Roe v. Wade case. The landmark Supreme Court decision that followed in fact decriminalized abortion nationwide, and in a certain sense, Nathanson and McCorvey had achieved victory.

But that's not the end of their stories. In the years following *Roe v. Wade*, their views on the issue of abortion changed dramatically. They eventually became vocal pro-life advocates, against abortion.

Just one year after the Roe decision, in a 1974 article, Dr. Nathanson expressed doubts that abortion was simply the removal of an "undifferentiated mass of cells." As ultrasound technology had emerged, Nathanson soon found it impossible to deny the humanity of the unborn child. He wrote, "I am deeply troubled by my own increasing certainty that I had in fact presided over 60,000 deaths." This self-identified Jewish atheist would begin a spiritual journey after befriending Father John McCloskey, an Opus Dei priest. He later converted to Catholicism and was baptized by Cardinal John O'Connor, archbishop of New York, in St. Patrick's Cathedral on December 8, 1996.

By this time, Norma McCorvey had begun her own path of conversion. In 1995, her life changed when a pro-life organization moved into an office next to the Dallas abortion clinic where she was working. Just a year earlier, she had published a book in which she chronicled her troubled childhood, substance abuse, three pregnancies, and her support of Roe v. Wade.

Within months of meeting her pro-life neighbors, Norma left the abortion industry forever and became an evangelical Christian. She was later received into the Catholic Church in 1998 by Father Frank Pavone, national director of *Priests for Life*. She also published a second book—a story of repentance, mercy, conversion and hope. Norma made a confession in a public service announcement: "My case, which legalized abortion on demand, was the biggest mistake of my life."

Norma McCorvey is another one of those Catholics who changed the world we live in, as is Dr. Nathanson, and so many others who helped people see the world with clearer eyes.

48

McLuhan, Marshall: Social Media

We see it happening all around us: technology is changing the world right before our eyes. But there is more to it—it is changing us as well. The Internet is changing the way we act, think, react and interact. Facebook and Twitter are doing the same. Cell phones are doing it too. All these new tools affect the way we live at home, at school, or at work. They have made us different from our parents, and the new generation is becoming different from the previous generation—for better or for worse. The outcome is paradoxical: with these new electronic devices, we are more connected than ever, and simultaneously, more disconnected than ever.

What we see happening here has been captured by the famous slogan "the medium is the message"—which means that a medium such as the current social media affects the society in which it plays a role, not so much by the content delivered over the medium, but by the characteristics of the medium itself. The man who coined and popularized this slogan was Marshal McLuhan (1911-1980).

Herbert Marshall McLuhan was born in Edmonton, Alberta, to Elsie Naomi (née Hall) and Herbert Ernest

McLuhan, both born in Canada. His mother was a Baptist school teacher who later became an actress; his father was a Methodist and had a real-estate business in Edmonton. Marshall studied at the University of Manitoba, Canada, and the University of Cambridge, England. He began his teaching career as a professor of English at several universities in the U.S. and Canada before moving to the University of Toronto in 1946, where he remained for the rest of his life. His work is considered one of the cornerstones in the study of media theory.

Many people may not know his name, but they do know his seemingly cryptic statement "the medium is the message." McLuhan pointed to the light bulb as a clear demonstration of this concept. A light bulb does not have content in the way that a newspaper has reports or a television has programs, yet it is a medium that has a social effect; that is, a light bulb enables people to create spaces during nighttime that would otherwise be enveloped by darkness. He describes the light bulb as a medium without any content. In McLuhan's own words, "a light bulb creates an environment by its mere presence."

Something similar could be said about our current social media. The Internet, for instance, creates new mental habits and new patterns of thought just by its presence alone. Anyone addicted to Facebook or Twitter understands what he meant: our tools aren't separate from us but rather interact with us and alter who we are and see ourselves. Interestingly enough, McLuhan is known for having predicted the World Wide Web almost 30 years before it was invented.

But what most people do not know is that McLuhan had very strong Catholic ties. While studying at Cambridge University, he took the first steps toward his eventual conversion to Roman Catholicism in 1937, after he had been reading the Catholic writer G. K. Chesterton (§17). In 1935, he wrote to his mother: "[H]ad I not encountered Chesterton, I would have remained agnostic for many years at least." At the end of March 1937, McLuhan completed what was a slow but total conversion process, when he was formally received into the Roman Catholic Church. Embracing Catholic Christianity was a life-changing step for McLuhan, who now attended Mass daily and arose at 4:00 or 5:00 every morning to read passages of Scripture in English, Italian, Spanish and French, and to ponder their meaning. For the rest of his career, he taught exclusively in Roman Catholic institutions of higher education.

It was this Catholic background that guided him in his further reflections on social media. Chesterton and Thomas Aquinas, he said, were his two biggest influences. Nearly forty years after his time in Cambridge, McLuhan said about Chesterton: "I know every word of him: he's responsible for bringing me into the church. He writes by paradox—that makes him hard to read (or hard on the reader)." He loved Chesterton's rhetorical trimmings, guzzled his playfulness, turned his impulse to try out new combinations of ideas into the hallmark of the McLuhan method.

From Aquinas (§60), McLuhan derived the belief that Catholicism entails what he termed "complete intellectual freedom to examine any and all phenomena with the absolute assurance of their intelligibility." McLuhan declared himself "a Thomist for whom the sensory order [the sensible world] resonates with the Divine Logos."

He explored further on this thought in the following reflections. "In Christ, Medium becomes message. Christ came to demonstrate God's love for man and to call all men to him through himself as Mediator, as Medium," he said once. "And in so doing he became the proclamation of his Church, the message of God to man. God's medium became God's message."

His book *The Medium Is the Message*, published in 1967, was McLuhan's bestseller, eventually selling nearly a million copies worldwide. It has been said that what Darwin was to biology, Marx to political science, Einstein to physics, and Freud to psychology, McLuhan was to communications studies. His core insight was basically a simple one: technology isn't just an external tool; it also changes how we think. Technology is changing the world right before our eyes. "The medium is the message" means that each new technology humanity has invented—from the wheel to the alphabet to the Internet—creates new mental habits and new patterns of thought. McLuhan confided to a friend his "terror" at the prospect facing civilization if men did not learn to understand the use and consequences of new media. How prophetic!

McLuhan's philosophy is founded on one key idea: we shape our environment, and it shapes us; we shape the tools, and the tools shape us. He also kept repeating that all media are "extensions" of our human senses, bodies and minds. Print culture, ushered in by the Gutenberg press in the middle of the fifteenth century (§34), brought about the cultural predominance of the visual over the aural/oral. According to McLuhan, the advent of print technology contributed to and made possible most of the salient trends in the modern period in the Western world: individualism, democracy, Protestantism, capitalism and nationalism.

However, a medium has its effects also on senses other than those with which it communicates. In the early 1960s, McLuhan wrote that the visual, individualistic print culture would soon be brought to an end by what he called "electronic interdependence"—that is, when electronic media replaces visual culture with aural/oral culture. As he put it, "Instead of tending towards a vast Alexandrian library the world has become a computer, an electronic brain." This was basically another anticipation of the upcoming "world-wide-web."

More controversial, however, is his idea that *content*, the message itself, has little effect on society—in other words, it wouldn't matter if television broadcasts children's shows or violent programming, for instance—the effect of television on society would be the same. There may be something to it, though. For years, debates have raged among scholars, politicians and concerned parents about the effects of media violence on viewers. Too often these debates have descended into simplistic battles between those who claim that media messages directly cause violence and those who argue that activists exaggerate the impact of media exposure altogether. The discussion has not been settled, although studies have repeatedly shown that those who watch the most television are likely to perceive the world as a more frightening and scary place than it actually is. Studies also show that children who watch a lot of violence accept it as a normal part of life.

McLuhan summed up his philosophy in the dictum that the medium is the message. Without a physical medium, there is no message; without a clear medium, there is no clear message. He applied this idea also to language itself. We have no access to thoughts and ideas except through the tool of language. The expression of ideas depends on a physical tool, language. Without language there is no expression of ideas and, without the right words, the expression of ideas is flawed and imperfect. Without the right words, there could be no correct expression of ideas.

Marshall McLuhan is another one of those Catholics who changed the world we live in, or at least the way we see the world. He became for many a communications guru who had an important message for the modern world.

49

Mendel, Gregor: Genetics

It has long been believed that a child "blends" features of both parents, as if it were a matter of mixing two kinds of blood. We think we see this happening, for instance, when a child with a black parent and a white parent has a skin color somewhere in-between. Currently, we no longer believe this kind of explanation. The story is quite a bit more complicated. We know now that what parents pass on to their children is not blood, but "genes" and "DNA."

When you ask geneticists nowadays who was the first one to talk about genes, they almost certainly come up with the name of Gregor Mendel (1822-1884). What did Mendel do for genetics?

Gregor Mendel was born as Johann Mendel in a German-speaking family in the Silesian part of the Austrian Empire (in Moravia, today's Czech Republic). He was given the name Gregor when he entered the Augustinian Abbey of St. Thomas in Brno (called Brünn in German). He was ordained a priest in 1847, and went to the University of Vienna for further studies. In 1854, he returned to the abbey and became a physics teacher at a school in Brünn, where he taught for the next 16 years. This was also the time where he would do his famous experiments on plant genetics in the "lab" of his monastery's garden. He ended up becoming abbot of the Abbey.

Mendel may have been practically unknown during his lifetime, but thanks to some geneticists after him, he has been heralded as "the father of genetics." For almost 35 years, Mendel's findings escaped notice, until other geneticists such as Hugo De Vries in Holland, Erich Von Tschermak in Austria, Carl Correns in Germany and William Bateson in England discovered similar results, independent from each other. When they came across Mendel's original paper from 1866, this helped them interpret their own data better. Correns would write later, "I thought that I had found something new. But then I convinced myself that the Abbot Gregor Mendel in Brünn, had... obtained the same result." Because of this, Mendel has been coined the founder of what soon became known as "Mendelism."

How was it possible that Mendel's revolutionary work in genetics was not noticed for such a long time? There are many possible explanations. Perhaps Mendel was operating on the fringes of the scientific community and published his article in an unknown, rather provincial journal. Then there is the possibility that rivalry and jealousy are to blame, for Mendel did send copies of his article to many colleagues, but they hardly reacted. Or perhaps Mendel's discoveries were "premature," because the time was not "ripe" yet for such revolutionary ideas until 35 years later.

Whatever the explanation is, Correns and Bateson got the impression Mendel had done already in 1865 what they were doing in 1900. The adjective "genetic" had already been used by Huxley as early as 1864, but Bateson adapted this 19th-century term to inaugurate a new science, which he named "genetics." He also phrased the new terminology of genetics and applied it to Mendel's findings.

According to this new terminology, Mendel had been working with two forms of the *gene* for seed shape—one that produced round peas and another one that produced wrinkled peas. From now on, when a gene exists in more than one form, the different forms are called *alleles*. When an organism contains two of the same alleles, it is called *homozygous*; if it contains two different alleles of the same gene, it is called *heterozygous*. If one allele is dominant (A) over the recessive one (a), visual inspection does not tell us whether the organism is homozygous for the dominant allele (AA) or rather heterozygous (Aa). Let's leave it at that.

We still speak of "Mendelian laws." They worked so well that they could be applied also to human blood types and blood groups (§42). Of course, it is not only blood group systems that follow Mendelian rules of inheritance. There are some serious diseases that may emerge when certain genes carry altered alleles. Several diseases are traceable to a single gene. What many of these diseases have in common is that they follow a simplified formula: one gene can lead to one specific disease if it carries an altered, dominant allele, or two altered recessive alleles. But there is much more to it of course. Examples like these give us an idea of how powerful Mendelian laws and rules have been for genetics and the medical sciences—not to mention for new developments in DNA-research.

Gregor Mendel is another one of those Catholics who changed the world we live in. He revolutionized the way we have come to understand genetics and the transfer of genes and DNA.

50

More, Thomas: Religious Liberty

"Religious liberty" is a rather murky concept that makes for a murky discussion. Is it about the freedom to discuss religion? If so, then G.K. Chesterton's remark comes to mind, "Religious liberty might be supposed to mean that everybody is free to discuss religion. In practice it means that hardly everybody is allowed to mention it."

Or is "freedom of religion" perhaps about the freedom to believe in anything you want? That sounds very democratic, but do we really want to protect "religions" such as "flying saucer cults," "Branch Davidians," or "Nuwaubianism," when they want to rule society life? If we compare this with freedom of speech, would we consider hate-speech protected also by freedom of speech? As a matter of fact, not all speech is of the same quality, neither are all religions.

Or is "freedom of religion" perhaps about the freedom to let your religion dictate what you can or should do in society? If so, we should realize that not all religions are of the same quality and don't have the same right to rule people's actions in society. Not all religions are created equal. Pope Benedict XVI even spoke of "sick and distorted forms of religion." Therefore, not all "religious beliefs" have a claim to our respect—especially not if they go against *reason* (§60). Religions based on extraterrestrial sources or on books that only some people are supposed to have access to or on books that have never been recovered anywhere have a hard time to pass the test of reason.

So there must be something else at stake in this discussion. Religion is not just about beliefs and opinions people have but about what is true or not true. Unfortunately, the concept of *truth* has become very shaky in recent times, and that's why the discussion about freedom of religion has become shaky as well.

Something is true, and only true, when our minds conform to what is out there, which is an affirming activity called "knowing the truth." Without it, we are lost. You cannot consistently claim that truth doesn't exist. If there is no truth beyond your belief that something is true or false, then you cannot hold your own beliefs to be true. Or if you believe that all truth is relative to one's frame of reference, you cannot at the same time claim that this belief itself is absolutely true, an exception to its own rule. Instead, the truth is that truth is truth, even if you do not accept it; and untruth is untruth, even if you claim it. Truth is truth for everyone, anywhere, at any time.

Therefore, we need some kind of deciding factor to determine which religious beliefs are true, and which are not. Well, this deciding factor is *reason*. Religious beliefs that are against reason cannot be true; religious faith that is not open to reason cannot be true; religions that are irrational and incoherent cannot be true (§41). The canons of reason are needed to weed out what is *not* plausible in what a certain religion tells us about God and morality.

Once we have clarified what "religious freedom" means, we can begin to defend our own religion by showing that it is not against reason, and only then can we validly defend our right to use this freedom of religion—which is actually a fight for the truth in defense of the truth. We can even become a martyr of the truth, and of the freedom of religion. The most exemplary case of such martyrdom is Thomas More (1478-1535).

Thomas More was born in London as the son of Sir John More, a successful lawyer and later judge, and his wife Agnes (née Graunger). He was the second of six children. More was educated at St Anthony's School, then considered one of London's finest schools. From 1490 to 1492, More served John Morton, the Archbishop of Canterbury and Lord Chancellor of England, as a household page. Believing that More had great potential, Morton nominated him for a place at the University of Oxford. So Thomas began his studies at Oxford in 1492, and received a classical education. He left Oxford after only two years—at his father's insistence—to begin legal training in London. After many other important assignments, More was assigned Lord Chancellor in 1529—the second highest seat of authority next to the king himself.

Soon after, the trouble would start for More when King Henry VIII attempted to receive an annulment for his marriage to Queen Catherine of Aragon. Although Henry cited the fact that Catherine was previously married to his deceased brother as giving him grounds for demanding an annulment, the real reason he sought an annulment was because she could not produce any lasting male heirs for his throne, and he had fallen in love with Anne Boleyn, Catherine's maid. Although Cardinal Wolsey, the highest ranking Catholic clergyman in England, was willing to grant the annulment, Pope Clement VII was not. The pontiff stuck to his guns and refused to acknowledge Henry's marriage to Catherine as anything but real.

After King Henry realized that Pope Clement would not change his mind, he inaugurated what is known as the "English Reformation" by means of a series of acts passed through the

50 More, Thomas: Religious Liberty

English Parliament. These acts—the chief one of which was the 1534 "Act of Supremacy"—recognized King Henry and his successors as the "Sole Protector and Supreme Head on earth of the Church and Clergy of England." This effectively made Henry the "pope" of England.

Not long after, King Henry forced parliament to take things one step further. He had them pass an "Act of Succession," which stated that Anne Boleyn's children would the rightful heirs to the English throne and that Henry's first marriage to Catherine was invalid and, therefore, annulled. In Henry's foolish wisdom, he even forced all Englishmen over the age of twenty-one to sign an oath swearing that they agreed to the Act of Succession. Naturally, the majority of the citizens caved in and signed it under the threat of treason.

But not so Thomas More. He refused to sign it. Rather than publicly opposing the King's marriage, which would have endangered his wife and children, More decided to resign his office as Chancellor of England and keep silent. But he refused to acknowledge the King's headship of the English Church. Because of his refusal, he was imprisoned, convicted of treason and beheaded. He approached his execution wearing his finest clothes and pronouncing loudly to the crowds, "I am dying for our Catholic faith, good people. And I call you to witness that I die the king's loyal servant—but God's first."

What, then, was Thomas More a martyr for? What all martyrs die for: truth. Thomas refused to support Henry's actions because they denied the truth about the sacrament of marriage, the teachings of the Church and of papal authority. He defended the right to defend the truth—that is to say, not just anything people call "truth," but the truth that has passed the test of reason. He was willing to die for the truth of his Catholic religion. He attacked the validity of the law he had been charged with breaking because it contradicted the words of Christ himself. Of course, we ought to be obedient to and follow the laws of our land, but like Augustine, Thomas Aquinas, and even Dr. Martin Luther King were so fond of saying, "An unjust law is no law at all." Freedom of religion gives us the right to say so.

Thomas More is commonly referred to as a "man for all seasons" because of his reputation as a scholar, politician, theologian, lawyer, the Lord High Chancellor of England, and, most importantly, a devoted Catholic. He had a formidable intellect, a strong sense of duty to his country and countrymen, a quick wit, a relentless humor, and a strong love of God and his Catholic Church.

Thomas More is considered relevant to our times because he was a martyr for religious liberty—that is, for defending the truth—which is now endangered by efforts to force Catholics in many countries to go against their religion on issues such as marriage, contraception, abortion and gender. The persecution that threatens Catholics today is also fundamentally about truth and love for the truth. Just like More faced death for refusing to support Henry's denial of papal authority, so do we face even the possibility of ostracism, imprisonment and financial penalties for refusing to support our society's denial of basic truths about contraception, marriage, abortion and gender. Thomas More is our champion.

Some tend to describe religious truths like these with political terms: the Church is said to have a "ban" on contraception, a "policy" against female ordination, a "rule" about euthanasia. This terminology is entirely unfitting—and misleading. Bans can be lifted. Policies can be altered. Rules can be changed. Truths cannot.

When we argue against laws that contradict "the laws of

God," just as More did, others will have to acknowledge that we have an objective, rational argument for our position, however much they may reject or disagree with it. Cardinal John Henry Newman said it right, "no man will be a martyr for a conclusion… he dies for realities." Likewise, More did not die for so abstract a notion as "liberty" but for very concrete truths about the basic truth of the Catholic religion.

Thomas More is another one of those Catholics who changed the world we live in. He showed the world that truth surpasses unjust laws. Laws can be man-made, truths are God-given.

51

Pasteur, Louis: Micro-organisms

People probably have always been aware of diseases that were caused by micro-organisms creating havoc by invading our bodies. But they didn't know they were caused by tiny invaders—so tiny that we can't even see them with the naked eye. Microscopes were needed to make those microbes visible. Yet, we have always instinctively avoided people infected with leprosy, typhus, cholera, tuberculosis, syphilis, and the list goes on and on. But for a very long time, we didn't even have any idea why.

The discovery of "micro-organisms" or "microbes" is essential to modern medicine. The fields of microbiology and immunology would be impossible without this knowledge. So many people would still be dying at a large scale, if we didn't know about these tiny, microscopic "invaders." We had been surrounded by them for centuries, or even millennia, without knowing they existed. We wonder where the idea came from that there are infectious micro-organisms which can be transferred from person to person. If you want to find the man who has contributed most to the saving of human lives from infectious diseases, you inevitably will come across Louis Pasteur (1822-1895).

51 Pasteur, Louis: Micro-organisms

Louis Pasteur was born in 1822, in Dole, Jura, France, to a Catholic family of a poor tanner. Louis was the third child of Jean-Joseph Pasteur and Jeanne-Etiennette Roqui. After he had finished his basic education and after many more years of study, Louis became professor of chemistry at the University of Strasbourg, where he met and dated Marie Laurent, daughter of the university's rector in 1849. They were married that year, and together had five children, only two of whom survived to adulthood; the other three died of typhoid.

In 1863, Pasteur was appointed professor of geology, physics and chemistry at the *École nationale supérieure des Beaux-Arts*, a position he held until his resignation in 1867 when he received a chair at the Sorbonne and was appointed director of a physiological chemistry laboratory, which was created at Pasteur's request. He was the laboratory's director from 1867 to 1888. In Paris, he established the *Pasteur Institute* which was his own private research facility. He was its director for the rest of his life.

Louis Pasteur started his work on micro-organisms with a very practical issue. He demonstrated that a tiny micro-organism in yeast is responsible for the fermentation of sugar into alcohol. He also demonstrated that, when a different micro-organism contaminates the wine, lactic acid is produced, making the wine sour. This led Pasteur to the idea that micro-organisms causing fermentation could also be the cause of certain diseases. Most likely, his personal tragedies caused by the death of three of his own children by typhoid motivated him strongly to find a cure for infectious diseases.

Having studied many cases of childbed fever, also called puerperal fever (§57), among pregnant women at the hospitals, he declared before a medical society that he had seen its cause: microbial predators. He drew a picture resembling a rosary of "berries," which we now know as a streptococcus, making for a chain of coccus microbes. He discovered other coccus forms of pathological microbes, some of them arranged in bunches like grapes, thence called staphylococci. He then proposed preventing the entry of micro-organisms into the human body, which would soon lead to antiseptic methods in surgery.

All of this was done while remaining a very devout Catholic. "The more I study nature, the more I stand amazed at the work of the creator," he said. He just could not understand the failure of some scientists to recognize the existence of the Creator in the world around them. Yet, he advocated separation of science and religion (§1). As he put it, "In each one of us there are two men, the scientist and the man of faith or of doubt. These two spheres are separate." Thus he advocated that the man of faith can be a co-worker in God's creation and thus can help mankind rise above disease and poverty by applying scientific principles in bio-medical research.

He died in 1895, with the rosary in his hand, after listening to the life of St. Vincent de Paul which he had asked to have read to him because he thought that his own work like that of St. Vincent would do much to save suffering children.

Louis Pasteur is another one of those Catholics who changed the world we live in. He helped humanity to identify "germs" and to keep them and their victims under control.

52

Paul of Tarsus: Apostle without Borders

Christianity was born in the cradle of Judaism. As Pope Pius XI once said about Christians, "Spiritually we are Semites." Not surprisingly, this raises many pertinent questions. Are the real Christians Jews or are they Gentiles? Are the real Christians circumcised Jews or uncircumcised Gentiles? Is the real Christianity based on the Old Covenant, or on the New Covenant instead? Is Christianity perhaps only a branch of Judaism? If that were true, one would have to be a Jew to be a Christian.

These are some of the questions in need of an answer. The man who played a key role in answering them is Paul of Tarsus (5-67).

Paul, whose original name was Saul, was born in Tarsus, in the country we now call Turkey. As a boy, he learned from his father the family business—making and repairing tents. Saul's parents were faithful Jews. They prayed that God would soon keep his promise to send the Messiah. When Saul was a young man, he was sent to Jerusalem to study Jewish law. When he returned home, he began to hear about a prophet named Jesus who claimed to be the Messiah whom his parents had prayed for. People said this man had risen from the dead and that he had worked miracles as a sign that he had been sent by God. But Saul didn't believe them. He began to persecute these Jesus' followers. He demanded that they give up their new faith. But no matter what he did, more and more people became followers of Christ. They even began to call themselves Christians (§37)!

The first time, Paul—still called Saul at the time—is mentioned in the Acts of the Apostles is at the stoning of Stephen, the first Christian martyr, who was actually a Greek-speaking, Hellenistic Jew: "They threw him [Stephen] out of the city, and began to stone him. The witnesses laid down their cloaks at the feet of a young man named Saul" (Acts 7:58). It was then that Saul would witness how the first Christian martyr, Stephen, had to deal with the tension between the Old Covenant and the New Covenant.

It shouldn't come as a surprise that some early Christians—those with a Jewish background—would consider any influence of the Hellenistic Gentiles on Christianity as a distortion of its original purity. These so-called "Judaizers" among the early Christians criticized other Christians for having come under "Hellenistic influence." But interestingly enough, those who reject any "Hellenistic influence" in Christianity do not realize that their claim itself is a statement that "Judaizes." As Rod Bennett puts it, "[I]t assumes that Christianity is a Jewish thing being exported to Greeks—and that the Greek element is alien to it, something to be tolerated at best. And yet the New Testament is written in Greek because it is for Greeks." As a matter of fact, the early Gospel message was spread orally, probably in Aramaic, but almost immediately also in Greek. Hellenistic elements were just an inevitable part of early Christianity. Stephen testifies to this.

The killing of Stephen unleashed a local persecution of

Christians, the first one in the history of the Church: "On that day, there broke out a severe persecution of the church in Jerusalem, and all were scattered throughout the countryside of Judea and Samaria, except the apostles" (Acts 8:1). Apparently, Christianity had been spreading from Jerusalem to neighboring regions. Therefore, Saul followed them and expanded his persecution of Christians to other places, notably to Damascus. It was on his way to persecute Christians in Damascus that Jesus appeared to him and redirected his life.

From this miraculous event on, Paul deeply believed Christ had commissioned him as an apostle to the Gentiles: "for the one who worked in Peter for an apostolate to the circumcised worked also in me for the Gentiles" (Gal. 2:8). In his Letter to the Galatians, for instance, Paul tells us that in Antioch, Peter once stopped eating with Gentiles in order to appease the sentiments of certain Jews visiting the city. This caused Paul, a Jew, to rebuke him publicly: "I said to Cephas in front of all, 'If you, though a Jew, are living like a Gentile and not like a Jew, how can you compel the Gentiles to live like Jews?'" (Gal. 2:14). And later on, he would have to say something similar to the Judaizers in Rome: "Does God belong to Jews alone? Does he not belong to Gentiles, too? Yes, also to Gentiles, for God is one and will justify the circumcised on the basis of faith and the uncircumcised through faith" (Rom. 3:29-30). Then he added emphatically: "For there is no distinction between Jew and Greek; the same Lord is Lord of all, enriching all who call upon him" (Rom. 10:12).

It was mostly Paul who changed the outlook of the first Christians dramatically. After Jesus' death, his followers had to face a pivotal question: how would the world know that he, the Messiah, was ever here? How would his work be preserved and continued? For this purpose, Jesus' disciples would bring their new message to all the corners of the Roman Empire. They would spread this new religion, Christianity, to all Roman citizens, Jew or Gentile alike. Initially, Christianity was considered a small branch of Judaism and therefore would experience a rather tolerant treatment. But things would change quickly. Suetonius, a non-Christian source about the Christians, refers to the expulsion of Jews by Emperor Claudius (41-54) and states, "Since the Jews constantly made disturbances at the instigation of Chrestus [sic], he expelled them from Rome." There was trouble brewing at the horizon.

It was the Apostle Paul who was more inclined than the Apostle Peter to be the bridge builder between Judaism and Hellenism. Although he realized that Jesus' mission was first of all to the Jews, he also knew the focus was shifting. Together with Barnabas, Paul spoke boldly to the Jews: "It was necessary that the word of God be spoken to you first, but since you reject it and condemn yourselves as unworthy of eternal life, we now turn to the Gentiles" (Acts 13:46).

What made things so difficult for Peter to accept this is the fact that the first Christians and their Scriptures were keen to express that Jesus' mission was first and foremost to Israel and the Jews. Given Jesus' rather exclusive mission to Israel, it took a while for the Early Church, most notably for Peter, to recognize that salvation was also available to the Gentiles without their converting to Judaism. Although the Jewish Christians who had fled the persecution in Jerusalem had gone into the Gentile regions of Phoenicia, Cyprus and Antioch, they were still "spreading the word only among Jews (Acts 11:19). Peter himself was also rather hesitant to bring the Gospel to the Gentile household of Cornelius, for instance, but God made it clear to him that Cornelius was also one of the elect (Acts 10).

Both Peter and Paul must have wondered what Jesus'

position was in this debate. On the one hand, Jesus tells us he was sent to the people of Israel first. He selected Jewish disciples, spoke in Jewish synagogues and the Jewish temple, and traveled mostly in Jewish territory. His mission, in fulfillment of the Jewish prophets, was to the Jewish people. On the other hand, none of this means that Jesus' ministry was limited exclusively to the Jews. He ministered to a Samaritan woman (Mk. 7:24-30). He spoke extensively with a Samaritan woman at the well (John 4:4_42). He healed a Roman centurion's servant (Lk. 7:1-10). He traveled through the Gentile region of the Gerasenes (Mk. 5:1). And before his Ascension into Heaven, he sent his disciples on a mission with these words: "you will be my witnesses in Jerusalem, throughout Judea and Samaria, and to the ends of the earth" (Acts 1:8). No doubt, Israel has a special place in God's salvation—it's Israel that God had prepared for the coming of the Messiah—but apparently not an exclusive role. Paul, in his missionary journeys, followed the same priority that Jesus had followed—that is, preaching to the Jews first (Rom. 1:16).

Does this mean, Christians had to become Jews first? Does this mean they had to be circumcised? Obviously, another miracle was needed. The Acts of the Apostles reports, "Some who had come down from Judea were instructing the brothers, 'Unless you are circumcised according to the Mosaic practice, you cannot be saved'" (Acts 15:1). This convinced Paul that he had to go to Jerusalem. During the meeting there, "some from the party of the Pharisees who had become believers stood up and said, 'It is necessary to circumcise them and direct them to observe the Mosaic law'" (Acts 15:50). Obviously, the Church needed to make an official decision about this issue—which she did during the first Church Council in Jerusalem.

The Council sent a circular letter to all Christians stating, "we have with one accord decided to choose representatives and to send them to you along with our beloved Barnabas and Paul" (Acts 15:25). The letter they carried was in force for all Christian communities: "As they traveled from city to city, they handed on to the people for observance the decisions reached by the apostles and presbyters in Jerusalem" (Acts 16:4). So, the Church had officially spoken.

Of all the apostles, the Apostle Paul can perhaps be given the greatest credit for this outcome. It was this new Church policy that made the Christian life more appealing to all the citizens of the Roman Empire, and thus enabled the Christianization throughout the West and eventually throughout the entire world. Without Paul, the Church would most likely not have spread with the rapidity that she did.

Paul of Tarsus is another one of those Catholics who changed the world we live in. He removed all the borders for Christianity and made it a "religion without borders."

53

Paul VI: Sexual Revolution

It has become a popular stance in our "civilized" society that men can follow all their sexual desires and that women can be free and truly own their own sexuality. That's considered civilized, a sign of progress.

In contrast, you might also think that the civilized world is becoming more and more uncivilized—with a devastating breakdown of marriage and family, a dramatic increase of single mothers, a staggering rise in broken families, a growing number of children living in poverty, an alarming surge in legalized killing of unborn babies. If you agree this is uncivilized, you may wonder what the cause is behind all of these shocking changes. Is there perhaps one particular factor that may explain all these seemingly disparate phenomena?

Many explanations have been suggested, but one of them seems to stick out as the underlying cause of all these new alarming developments—it is the so-called Sexual Revolution. Just open the newspaper or turn on the television, and you will see what the Sexual Revolution has done for us. It has been repeatedly stated that the major cause of the breakdown of the family is the Sexual Revolution, and the major cause of the

Sexual Revolution is the Pill. The person who was arguably the first one to expose this concealed connection was Pope Paul VI (1897-1978).

Paul VI was born Giovanni Battista Montini in the village of Concesio, in the province of Brescia, Lombardy, Italy. His father, Giorgio Montini, was a lawyer, journalist, director of the Catholic Action, and member of the Italian Parliament. His mother was Giudetta Alghisi, from a family of rural nobility. In 1916, he entered the seminary to become a Catholic priest. He was ordained on May 29, 1920, in Brescia. Montini concluded his studies in Milan with a doctorate in Canon Law in the same year. Afterwards he studied at the Gregorian University. His organizational skills led him soon to a career in the Roman Curia. Seen as the most likely successor to Pope John XXIII—because of his pastoral and administrative background, his insight and determination, and his closeness to both Popes Pius XII and John XXIII—Montini was elected pope in 1963.

Perhaps the most important, but also most controversial, encyclical of his eight encyclicals was *Humanae vitae*, issued in 1968, in which he made the connection between the crises of modern society and the rise of the Sexual Revolution, more in particular birth control. The Sexual Revolution was just beginning and many Catholics expected the Church to get on the bandwagon. But Pope Paul predicted what would happen if birth control did become a widespread phenomenon. Therefore, *Humanae vitae* was vilified by some and highly praised by others.

The pontiff's words were so prophetic that only time could tell how accurate his assessment of the situation was. Now that fifty years have passed, we can see that what some called Pope Paul's "blindness" was rather prophetic insight, and his "stubbornness" was pastoral fortitude. He was "stubborn" in

53 Paul VI: Sexual Revolution

defending the Church's role in society—to transform the culture, not to be transformed by the culture. And at the same time he was "prophetic." Fifty years ago, he "prophesied" that marriages and society would suffer if the use of contraception would become widespread due to the Sexual Revolution. What was it that made his encyclical so prophetic? Pope Paul made four rather general "prophecies" about what would happen if the Church's teaching on contraception were ignored.

(1) The pontiff first noted that the widespread use of contraception would "lead to conjugal infidelity and the general lowering of morality." These two things go hand in hand; one not need look further than the dramatic increase in divorce, abortion and sexually transmitted diseases since 1968. The pontiff affirmed that "children are really the supreme gift of marriage," and he went on to predict that any society that abandoned such a concept would eventually unravel. He foresaw clearly that the right to contraception leads to the right of abortion, and the choice of abortion gives fathers the choice to marry or not. The actual increase in the number of divorces, abortion, out-of-wedlock pregnancies and venereal diseases should convince any skeptic that sexual morality is not the strong suit of our age. The idea that mankind at last had found the scientific and technical means to control human fertility has been blown to pieces.

(2) Pope Paul also argued that "the man" will lose respect for "the woman" and "no longer [care] for her physical and psychological equilibrium" and will come to "the point of considering her as a mere instrument of selfish enjoyment and no longer as his respected and beloved companion." Sex became merely a recreational tool. To see what this did, all we have to do is look at the explosion in pornography, sex trafficking, exploitation of women in Hollywood and in so many

other places. Porn leads men to see fewer and fewer women as "'porn-worthy." In the pope's words, "A man who grows accustomed to the use of contraceptive methods may forget the reverence due to a woman, and, disregarding her physical and emotional equilibrium, reduce her to being a mere instrument for the satisfaction of his own desires, no longer considering her as his partner whom he should surround with care and affection." We end up with a generation of men who whine and manipulate when they don't get sex on demand.

(3) Pope Paul also observed that the widespread acceptance of contraception would place a "dangerous weapon... in the hands of those public authorities who take no heed of moral exigencies." The history of the family-planning programs in the Third World is a sobering testimony to this reality. Contraception and abortion have not liberated women at all, as they were supposed to, but instead enslaved them to chemicals that distort the natural functions of their bodies and to grisly surgical procedures that can leave them scarred for life both physically and emotionally. The World Health Organization has placed the estrogen-progestogen pill on its list of Group 1 carcinogens—the most toxic rating it can impose, together with tobacco and asbestos. As a matter of fact, hormonal contraceptives have been tied to strokes, heart attacks, lupus, inflammatory bowel disease, reduced immunity and increased susceptibility to sexually transmitted diseases. More generally, it could be stated that humanity doesn't seem to be much happier because of the contraceptive revolution and the social culture it created. Nevertheless, due to a well-oiled and heavily-funded public relations campaign of the pharmaceutical industry, the Pill has been heralded as an important tool for women's liberty and women's "health" by plainly ignoring its side effects. The Pill has been heralded as the latest miracle

53 Paul VI: Sexual Revolution

cure.

(4) Pope Paul's final warning was that contraception would lead humans to think that they had unlimited dominion over their own bodies. Sterilization is now the most widely used form of contraception in the USA; individuals are so convinced of their rights to control their own bodies that they do not hesitate to alter even their own physical, sexual make-up. The false notion that man is his own creator and can be and can do whatever he wants sexually has also enabled the transgender and in-vitro movements. The Pill has in fact enabled the Sexual Revolution, and now in turn, the Sexual Revolution has revolutionized our ideas about sex and sexuality.

Almost everything that the Sexual Revolution promised us has been shattered. More and more statistics show this gloomy truth. Pope Paul VI should be lauded as one of the greatest sociologists of the 20th century. He was the great dissenter from the radically new sexual orthodoxy. A wealth of social science data has confirmed his assessment that the Sexual Revolution is bad for women, men and children alike—and the Pill has served as its enabler. This "revolution" has only led to growing numbers of children who are sexually abused and women who are beaten, abandoned or raped by men who do not want to hear about self-control and who consider every subject they meet as a mere object for their own use or abuse.

The fact that sex can result in a pregnancy has been the most powerful reason for centuries that minimally responsible people have waited until marriage to have sex. Once that possibility has become null and void, people have sex outside of marriage, babies are born outside of marriage, people prepare poorly for marriage and marriages break up at the snap of a finger, etc. Men, women and children alike are all losers in this scenario. As Peter Kreeft remarks, "[S]ocieties have survived with very bad political systems and very bad economies, but not without strong families."

However, statistics also show that few Catholics live by Pope Paul's teachings, and it seems safe to suppose that few Catholics have actually read *Humanae vitae*. Currently, 99% of Catholic obstetricians, gynecologists and family practitioners prescribe contraceptives. As medical doctors, they certainly know what *can* be done, but apparently not what *ought* to be done. They know more about biology than about morality because the latter subject is usually not taught at medical schools, which makes them think that everything biologically possible is therefore morally permissible. Pope Paul VI has news for them.

Pope Paul VI is another one of those Catholics who changed the world we live in. Pope Francis said about him that he "had the courage to stand against this majority, to defend moral discipline, to exercise a cultural brake." That's what modern society sometimes needs.

54

Pius XII: Not Hitler's Pope

How do you identify evil when you are confronted with it? That's not as easy as you might think—perhaps in hindsight, but not in foresight. A good example is Nazism. Not too many people saw the evil coming. Arthur Chamberlain, the Prime Minister of the UK, missed it; Joseph Kennedy, US Ambassador to the UK and the father of a future US president, missed it, as did many others. But there was definitely one exception: Pope Pius XII (1876-1958).

Pius XII was born Eugenio Maria Giuseppe Giovanni Pacelli in Rome into a family of intense Catholic piety with a history of ties to the papacy—the so-called "Black Nobility." His parents were Filippo Pacelli and Virginia (née Graziosi) Pacelli. His grandfather, Marcantonio Pacelli, had been Under-Secretary in the Papal Ministry of Finances and then Secretary of the Interior under Pope Pius IX from 1851 to 1870 and had helped found the Vatican newspaper, *L'Osservatore Romano* in 1861.

Pacelli was ordained a priest on Easter Sunday, 1899. By 1904, Pacelli received his doctorate. The theme of his thesis was the nature of concordats and the function of canon law when a concordat becomes inactive or suspended. He became an expert on concordats. Such concordats allowed the Church to organize youth groups, make ecclesiastical appointments, run schools, hospitals and charities, or even conduct religious services.

In 1914, he represented the Vatican when the Serbian Concordat was signed. In 1920, a Bavarian Concordat was completed. A Prussian Concordat was signed in 1929. When Pope Pius XI appointed him Cardinal Secretary of State in 1930, Pacelli became responsible for foreign policy and state relations throughout the world. In that function, he signed concordats with a number of countries and states: Austria (1933), Germany (1933), Yugoslavia (1935) and Portugal (1940).

The most controversial concordat was between the Catholic Church and Hitler's Germany. On July 20, 1933, Pius XI signed a concordat with Hitler, prepared by Pacelli who had been a nuncio in Germany from 1917 to 1929, before Hitler came into power. While attacked today as a Catholic capitulation to the Nazis, the concordat was viewed in its time in terms similar to those of the concordat of 1800 with Napoleon, and the many other more recent concordats—a treaty to protect the Church, not a surrender to the State (§32).

Interestingly enough, the initiative for the treaty did not come from the Vatican this time, but from Hitler, who wanted to remove Catholic clergymen from party politics. Franz von Papen, a Nazi in Catholic garb, was sent to Rome to conclude this pact, but received a cool reception from the now Secretary of State Pacelli, who was fully aware of how little faith could be placed in Hitler's promises.

When a new negotiator was sent to Rome again, Cardinal Pacelli continued to refuse agreement to the withdrawal of clergy from political activity until it became clear that the Catholic Center Party in Germany was about to dissolve itself as the last German party to hold out against Hitler. Then things moved quickly. The concordat was initialed in Rome on July 8, 1933. It was utterly clear the concordat was meant to protect Catholics in Germany, but certainly not Hitler. It was also utterly clear that this concordat with Hitler had nothing to do with anti-Semitism; in 1938, Pope Pius XI memorably declared that, in his own words, "anti-Semitism is a movement in which we Christians can have no part whatsoever…. Spiritually we are Semites."

Events like these probably explain why many people know Pius XII as "Hitler's Pope." However, this portrayal is a lie, in fact a vicious fabrication made up by the British writer and journalist John Cornwell. In his 1999 book entitled *Hitler's Pope*, Cornwell suggests that Pacelli, the pope-to-be, had visited Hitler, when in fact, Pacelli never set foot on Nazi soil after he left Germany for good in 1929—which is four years before Hitler obtained power. As a matter of fact, Pius XII never even met Hitler, much less collaborated with him. The two were relentless opponents.

Strangely enough, the photograph on the front cover of the American edition of Cornwell's book was manipulated to give the impression Pius was leaving from a visit to Hitler in March 1939, the month that Pacelli was made pope, when, in fact, the photo had been taken in 1927, before Hitler had taken over, as Pius was leaving a reception for German President von Hindenburg.

Not only did Pius XII speak out against Hitler and the Holocaust, he was one of the first ones to do so, authorizing Vatican Radio to explicitly condemn Nazi atrocities against Jews and Catholics in Poland, and personally confronting German Foreign Minister Joachim Ribbentrop over them. Robert Kempner, a prosecutor at the post-war Nuremberg

Tribunal, publicly praised Pius XII for having issued countless protests against German war crimes.

Pope Pius XII was in fact heavily and personally involved with the protection of Jews. An event that has been overshadowed the most by the pope's distorted image took place on October 16, 1943—famously called "Black Saturday." In the early hours of that day, occupying Nazi troops descended upon Rome's Jews, estimated to be at least 8,000. Although the ruthless Nazis were able to round up more than 1,200 Jews during Black Saturday, and would deport more than 1,000 of these to the Auschwitz-Birkenau extermination camp in Poland, the vast majority of them—some 85%—survived. They were being hidden and protected in Church-run institutions with Pius XII's knowledge, but most of all his support. The pope even opened up his own summer residence at Castel Gandolfo to take in Jews targeted for death. As the U.S. Holocaust Memorial Museum notes: "For every Jew caught by the Germans in Rome, at least ten escaped and hid, many in the Vatican."

The event has been immortalized in the well-known movie *The Scarlet and the Black.* Regrettably, the movie creates the impression that Monsignor Hugh O'Flaherty, the main player in the movie (played by Gregory Peck), acted on his own, without any guidance from Pope Pius XII. However, writings of and memories about the Monsignor have revealed that he was acting on the orders of Pius XII, whom O'Flaherty loyally, wholeheartedly, and enthusiastically served.

The same can be said about another underground network, portrayed in the movie *The Assisi Underground.* In September 1943, Fra Ruffino Niccacci was the Guardian of the Franciscan Monastery of San Damiano in Assisi. At the direction of Bishop Placido Nicolini and Aldo Brunacci, secretary to the bishop and chairman of the Committee to Aid Refugees, Padre Ruffino provided Jews with false identity cards and gave them sanctuary in local monasteries and convents. Again, the orders to do so came ultimately from the Vatican.

What also testified to this is the fact that Pius XII was widely praised for what he did during World War II. Commenting on the pope's 1942 Christmas address, the *New York Times* called the pope "a lonely voice crying out of the silence of a continent." Chaim Weizmann, who would become Israel's first President, wrote in 1943 a letter in which he offered thanks for "the support the Holy See was giving to lend its powerful help whenever it can to mitigate the fate of my coreligionists." In a similar vein, Winston Churchill called the pope "the greatest man of our time."

The same happened at Pius XII's death on October 9, 1958. It took the *New York Times* days to print the tributes from New York City rabbis alone. And Israel's Foreign Minister Golda Meir said, "In a generation afflicted by wars and discords, he upheld the highest ideals of peace and compassion." Similar sentiments were expressed by Rome's Chief Rabbi, Israel Zolli. One of Zolli's successors, the Chief Rabbi of Rome, Elio Toaff, said the same.

But matters would change soon. The framing of Pope Pius XII had begun as early as June 3, 1945, when Radio Moscow mendaciously alleged that he was "Hitler's Pope." This set a whole train of events into action, eventually culminating in the production of the stage play entitled *The Deputy* ("Der Stellvertreter" in German) by the then 32-year old German playwright Rolf Hochhuth.

There was a clear connection between this play and the Soviet campaign of defaming Pius XII. A first indication of a wider plot was the fact that the play was translated into more than twenty languages by translators who all "happened" to be Western communists or sympathizers. Interestingly enough, the first producer of the play, Erwin Piscator, had joined the German Communist Party in 1919 and had worked for Soviet intelligence in Moscow during World War II.

Most recently, General Ion Pacepa, a former high-level official in Romania's Communist dictatorship of Ceausescu and the highest-ranking official ever to defect from the Soviet Union, has given us details about the Soviet plot to defame Pius XII. Pacepa revealed that he himself had played an important role in this "disinformation" machinery and that he had sent Romanian agents to the Vatican disguised as priests. They gained access to the archives, copied and falsified documents, which were then made available to Hochhuth, who was doing "research" in Rome. Though it was an old Soviet plot, its misinformation has left an indelible mark on the minds of many.

Pope Pius XII is another one of those Catholics who changed the world we live in. The world is still grateful that he exposed the evil of Hitler and his Nazi ideology.

55

Ryan, John Augustan: Minimum Wage

Most people in Western Civilization live nowadays in what is called a "welfare state"—a concept of government in which the State plays a key role in the protection and promotion of the common good. When we "pay" the State for what the State does for us, we aren't paying for a service like the one a plumber delivers. When you pay the plumber, you expect service. If the plumbing is not fixed, you don't pay. But paying taxes to the State is not paying for a service—it's payment for the common good, and the State distributes it as best as it can to serve the common good. So we can't say we want our money back because we pay for some things we never use ourselves.

The welfare state involves a transfer of funds from the State to certain amenities such as healthcare, education, etc., as well as directly to individuals in the form of "benefits." All of this is funded through taxation. It is based on three principles: the principle of equality of opportunity, the principle of equitable distribution of wealth, and the principle of public responsibility for those unable to avail themselves of the minimal provisions needed for a decent life. Thus it combines democracy, welfare and capitalism.

One of the elements in a welfare state is the concept of a

minimum wage. That concept is so basic and generally accepted nowadays that it is hard to believe it hasn't always existed. As a matter of fact, it had to be "invented." The person who played an important role in this process is John Augustan Ryan (1869-1945).

John Augustan Ryan was born in Vermillion, Minnesota, to a large Irish family of Minnesota farmers. He attended secondary school at the Christian Brothers School in 1887. He chose to become a priest at age eighteen and attended St. Paul's Seminary nearby, now named the University of St. Thomas. During that time, Ryan read Pope Leo XIII's encyclical *Rerum novarum* (§44) in which he found Leo's statement that all laborers had a right to adequate worldly goods in order to live in frugal comfort, and that the State was obliged to guarantee that right.

He graduated valedictorian of his class in 1892. Graduating in 1898, Ryan was ordained by Archbishop John Ireland. With Ireland's permission, he then moved to Washington, D.C., to pursue graduate studies at the Catholic University of America that same year. There, Ryan received his Doctorate of Sacred Theology in 1906. His Ph.D. dissertation was an influential early economic and moral argument for minimum wage legislation. It was published with the title *A Living Wage*. Ryan insisted in the book that all men had a right to a "living wage," adequate to support themselves and their families. Always grounding his political thought in moral theology, Ryan argued that *Rerum novarum* converted the living wage "from an implicit to an explicit principle of Catholic ethics."

One of Ryan's inspirations, Richard Ely, recognized his dissertation as an authoritative moral and scientific analysis of the "living wage" concept introduced in *Rerum novarum*. The concept of a living wage described the need for all those who work to receive a fair wage from their employers which would enable them to sustain themselves and their families. Ely helped Ryan publish his dissertation, which was then translated into multiple languages. It stressed the right for a living wage as a natural right that exists from birth, rather than an entitlement given by the government.

Ryan saw himself as someone interested in Catholic social teaching based on right reason and informed by economic knowledge. His argument for a minimum wage was Ryan's most well-known contribution to American economic thought. He also viewed the separation of economic thought from religious and ethical rules as the root of practical economic problems faced by citizens in the early half of the twentieth century.

He returned to Washington where he served as a professor at the Catholic University from 1915 until 1939, teaching graduate level courses in moral theology, industrial ethics and sociology. During his tenure at the Catholic University, Ryan also taught economics and social ethics at Trinity College in Washington, now known as Trinity Washington University.

John Augustan Ryan is another one of those Catholics who changed the world we live in. He prepared the way for what we consider basic now—minimum wage. It was this Catholic priest who came up with the economic principles for a "living wage" and a "just wage," which later became the reality of the minimum wage, as we know it today.

56

Schumacher, E.F.: Small Is Beautiful

Many people these days live in a time of euphoria. Mass production methods have been generating more and cheaper goods than ever before. It has been a time of creating bigger markets and bigger political entities—culminating in unification projects such as the World Bank and the European Union. The power of global multinationals and of huge financial institutions has begun to take over. The buzzword is "globalization," the idea that "bigger is better," linked to another idea, "too big to fail."

But it's not all euphoria. The flipside is that the worker has become an anonymous cog in a huge machine. The economic system is making decisions on the basis of profitability rather than personal human needs. Companies that tried to stay small were soon snaffled up by corporate giants in their pursuit of larger and larger mergers. No wonder we yearn for economic systems within our control, that once again provide space for human interaction—for instance, farmers' markets and local cafes baking homemade cupcakes. Is there a way back, or is it a one-way, no-return ticket? A powerful voice in this call for a turnaround is Ernst Friedrich "Fritz" Schumacher (1911-1977).

E.F. Schumacher was a German-born, British statistician

and economist. He grew up in Bonn, Germany. His father was a professor of political economy. His sister, Elizabeth, was the wife of the physicist Werner Heisenberg. The younger Schumacher studied in Bonn and Berlin, then from 1930 in England as a Rhodes Scholar at New College, Oxford, and later at Columbia University in New York City, earning a degree in economics.

Schumacher moved back to England before World War II, as he had no intention of living under Nazism. He soon captured the attention of John Maynard Keynes, the founder of Keynesian economics, who found a position for him at Oxford University. After the War, Schumacher worked as an economic advisor to, and later Chief Statistician for, the British Control Commission, which was charged with rebuilding the German economy. From 1950 to 1970, he was Chief Economic Adviser to the National Coal Board, one of the world's largest organizations, with 800,000 employees.

Then, in 1973, he published his book *Small Is Beautiful: A Study of Economics As If People Mattered*. It was ranked by *The Times Literary Supplement* in 1995 as one of the 100 most influential books published after World War II. The phrase "Small Is Beautiful" came from a phrase by his teacher Leopold Kohr. Schumacher used it to champion small, appropriate technologies that are believed to empower people more than conglomerates, in stark contrast with phrases such as "Bigger is Better."

How did Schumacher come to his revolutionary insights? As a young man, Schumacher was a dedicated atheist, but beginning in the late 1950s, Catholicism heavily influenced his thinking. He was helped on his path to Rome by C.S. Lewis (§45). Schumacher also noted the similarities between his own economic views and the teaching of papal encyclicals on socio-economic issues, from Leo XIII's *Rerum novarum* (§0) to Pope John XXIII's *Mater et magistra*, as well as with the *subsidiarity* principle supported by Catholic thinkers such as G.K. Chesterton (§17) and Hilaire Belloc.

Not incidentally, Schumacher converted to Catholicism two years before his famous book appeared. The idea of appropriate technology has everything to do with the Catholic concept of subsidiarity. Subsidiarity calls for simple, local problem-solving whenever possible. It locates the responsibilities and privileges of social life in the smallest unit of organization at which they will function. Things are best done, in other words, at the smallest appropriate scale. As Schumacher would say later, "Any intelligent fool can make things bigger, more complex and more violent. It takes a touch of genius—and a lot of courage—to move in the opposite direction."

Schumacher's vision wasn't that everything should be small and local, but that in all things, ranging from decision-making in firms, to growing and distributing food and generating energy, our default position should be toward human scale. In this, the distance between decision and outcome, between production and consumption, is kept as short as usefully and practically possible.

Schumacher is another one of those Catholics who changed the world we live in. He had an important influence upon changing our perceptions of the world—and therefore, in some way, changing the world from "bigger is better" to "small is beautiful."

57

Semmelweis, Ignaz: Washing Hands

We all know these days how important it is to wash our hands frequently. In hospitals, antibiotic-resistant strains of bacteria can be wiped out by the simple act of hand-washing. Wards are supplied with antiseptic hand gel for medical staff and visitors to use before they see patients who are vulnerable to infection. The routine of "scrubbing up" by surgeons before an operation is, of course, a well-established practice to avoid infections. And during epidemics, we remind each other to frequently wash hands and avoid direct contact.

It won't come as a surprise that this has not always been that way. Until the late 1800s, surgeons of the time did not scrub up before surgery or even wash their hands between patients, thus causing infections to be transferred from one patient to another. Doctors and medical students in the maternity wards, for instance, routinely moved from dissecting corpses to examining new mothers without first washing their hands, thus causing death by "puerperal" or 'childbed' fever as a consequence. As anatomical, pathological dissection became more important to medical practice in the 1800s, the risk of infecting new mothers only got greater.

Strange as it may sound, the idea of surgeons washing their

hands is only 150 years old. Until then, all hospitals were pools of filth. Surgeons loved to speak of the "good old surgical stink" and took pride in the stains on their unwashed operating gowns as a sign of their experience. The man who discovered the need for surgeons, and others, to wash their hands was Ignaz Semmelweis (1818-1865).

Semmelweis was born Ignaz Philippe in Buda, Hungary, which in 1837 was combined with Pest to form Budapest. He was the fifth child born to Teresia Müller and Josef Semmelweis, both Catholic immigrants to Hungary from Germany. His parents were storekeepers that earned enough money to give their eight children an education. Growing up, Semmelweis spoke German at home instead of Hungarian. Semmelweis attended grammar school in Buda, and he finished his primary education at the Catholic Gymnasium of Buda in 1835. After his primary education, Semmelweis left Buda in 1837 to study law at the University of Vienna in Austria. But he quickly switched to medicine, completing his degree in 1844 and becoming accredited in midwifery, or the delivery of newborn babies, that same year.

Although some have claimed he was Jewish, the name Semmelweis itself is Swabian, and most assuredly not Jewish. Traceable through parish registers, the identities of Semmelweis' direct forebears are known, beginning with the birth and baptism of his great-great-grandfather, Gyorgy Semmelweis, in 1670. His family, like many middle-class Hungarians, was German-speaking and Catholic. His first name, Ignaz or Ignatius, couldn't be more Catholic (§37 and §38). One of his brothers became a Catholic priest. Like his ancestors, Semmelweis too was born and died a Roman Catholic.

At age 30, he was made assistant to the director of one of

57 Semmelweis, Ignaz: Washing Hands

two maternity clinics at Vienna General Hospital, which was the world's largest and most famous hospital at the time. His duties were to examine patients each morning in preparation for the professor's rounds, supervise difficult deliveries, teach students of obstetrics, and be "clerk" of records.

The hospital housed two obstetric clinics, the first for teaching medical students, the second for training midwives. Maternity institutions had been set up all over Europe, free of charge, and offered to care for the infants, which made them attractive to underprivileged women, including prostitutes. In return for free services, the women would be subjects for the training of doctors and midwives.

Semmelweis soon discovered an odd statistic in the records: maternal mortality rates at the first clinic, where the students were trained, had twice or sometimes three times the rate of the midwife-staffed second clinic. The leading cause of maternal mortality was what we consider now a serious bloodstream infection, called puerperal of childbed fever. To explain the difference, Ignaz tried eliminating various possibilities, from the position of giving birth to eliminating a walk-through by a priest after patients died—but with no evidence. He excluded "overcrowding" as a cause, since the Second Clinic was always more crowded, and yet the mortality was lower. After eliminating various other variables, Semmelweis was left with the conclusion that the only significant difference between the two clinics was the staff. But why did the medical students, with superb academic training, have a greater mortality rate than the midwives who had not the benefit of academic training?

In 1847, his close friend, Jakob Kolletschka, cut his finger while doing an autopsy. Kolletschka soon died of symptoms similar to those of puerperal fever. This led Semmelweis to note that the doctors and medical students were used to performing autopsies, while the midwives did not. So he came to a simple conclusion: the medical students also worked with cadavers, whereas the midwives had no such contact. The medical students took no hygienic steps between working on cadavers and delivering babies, and often used the same instruments for both activities. So he theorized that "particles" from the cadavers were responsible for transmitting the disease.

When Semmelweis realized this, he instituted a procedure requiring the students and staff at the first clinic—between autopsy work and the examination of patients—to wash their hands with a chlorine-based solution. Within a month, the mortality rate at the first clinic dropped to the same level as at the midwife clinic. The mortality rate in the first clinic had in fact dropped by 90%, and was then comparable to that in the second clinic.

Semmelweis had solved the problem! He lectured publicly about his results in 1850. But doctors weren't thrilled. For one thing, they were upset because Semmelweis' hypothesis made it look like they were the ones giving childbed fever to the women. Semmelweis had to spend 14 years developing and promoting his ideas, including publishing a poorly-reviewed book in 1861. Even the simplest understanding of Semmelweis' accomplishment drew scorn and ridicule in the medical community. Eventually, the doctors gave up the chlorine hand-washing, and Semmelweis lost his job. From now on, ignorance had become premeditated murder.

His Catholic upbringing had probably given him a strong sense of compassion, responsibility and duty for women who died in droves needlessly. It "made me so miserable that life seemed worthless," he said. He now realized that some kind of infection of the uterus or genital tract of women after childbirth was the cause of puerperal fever or childbed fever. This

57 Semmelweis, Ignaz: Washing Hands

explained to him what happened to, on average, 6 to 9 women in every 1000 deliveries, killing 2 to 3 of them with blood infections. It was the single most common cause of maternal mortality, accounting for about half of all deaths related to childbirth, and was second only to tuberculosis in killing women of childbearing age. This awareness drove Semmelweis to enforce his strict regimen of hand-washing relentlessly.

But that same Catholic upbringing had also given him a strong sense of distress and guilt. Semmelweis identified his own deadly contribution to the mortality of childbed fever. As he wrote later, "Only God knows the number of patients who went prematurely to their graves because of me." Over the years, Semmelweis got more frantic and even began to act strangely. Semmelweis was outraged by the indifference of the medical profession and began writing open and increasingly heated letters to prominent European obstetricians, in which he wrote, "I declare you a murderer before God and the world."

In 1865, when he was only 47 years old, he suffered a nervous breakdown and was committed to a mental asylum. The sad end of the story is that Semmelweis was probably beaten in the asylum by the guards and eventually died of an infection in the bloodstream—basically the same disease he had fought so hard to prevent in those women who died from childbed fever. So the irony is he himself died from blood poisoning. Semmelweis was buried in Vienna on August 15, 1865.

Semmelweis' upbringing probably had been the driving force for his success, but also for his downfall. Did he really change the world? Not really. For many more years, the medical community would persist in ignoring his findings and even ridiculing them. An added problem for Semmelweis was that his results lacked scientific explanation at the time. That became only possible some decades later, when Louis Pasteur (§51), Joseph Lister, and others developed the germ theory of disease. Only then did Semmelweis' practice earn widespread acceptance, years after his death, when Joseph Lister, acting on Louis Pasteur's confirmed germ theory, practiced and operated with great success, using hygienic methods of washing hands and sterilizing equipment. But even today, convincing health care providers that they should wash their hands often remains a challenge.

Yet, though not widely accepted and recognized for his findings, Semmelweis was the first one in history to realize the importance of washing procedures, not only for hands but also for surgical tools. His life and work have been widely used for films and books. Only slowly, too slowly, others would follow him.

Ignaz Semmelweis is another one of those Catholics who changed the world we live in. One might even call him a pioneer of and a "martyr" for the case of our current antiseptic policy.

58

Serra, Junípero: One Human Race

If you live in California or have ever been there, you must have wondered about all those names of towns starting with "San." Just think of names such as San Andreas, San Bernardino, San Bruno, San Diego, San Francisco, San Jose, San Leandro, San Luis Obispo, San Mateo and San Rafael. Some others start with "Santa," such as Santa Barbara and Santa Clara. *San* and *Santa* are the respective masculine and feminine translations for "Saint" in Spanish. Many of these names trace their origin back to missions that were founded by one man in particular: Junípero Serra (1713-1784).

Serra was born on the Spanish island of Majorca. His parents, Antonio Nadal Serra and Margarita Rosa Ferrer, spent their lives working the land in the town of Petra. He was only 15 years old when he decided to become a priest. After joining the Franciscans, Serra devoted much of his time to teaching. In 1742, he earned his doctorate in theology and then held for five years the Duns Scotus Chair of Philosophy at Lullian University in Majorca.

In 1749, Serra took on a new challenge—bringing his faith

to the New World as a missionary. He traveled first to Mexico, where he landed in Vera Cruz and then walked 250 miles to Mexico City. Along the way, he suffered an injury to his leg, which would cause him pain the rest of his life. He volunteered for the Sierra Gorda missions in 1751, which were located in the lands of Pame Indians. Serra preached to the native people and sought ways to improve the area's economy. He decided that to bring the natives to Christ, he would have to become one of them. So he mastered their language, treated them as equals, and daily worked side-by-side in their fields.

In 1769, Serra began his journey northward where he would do some of his best-known work: starting the California Missions. He established his first mission in San Fernando. Moving farther north, he founded another mission in San Diego, the first of nine missions he created in what is present-day California. Serra spent the rest of his life devoted to his evangelical work in the region. His attempts to bring Christianity to the Native Americans sometimes led to clashes with his own government. He clashed with Spanish authorities over the way soldiers treated the native peoples.

The Franciscan missions were designed not only to bring the Catholic faith to the native peoples, but also to integrate them into Spanish society, and to train them to take over ownership and management of the land. As head of the Franciscans in California, Serra not only dealt with church officials, but also with Spanish officials in Mexico City and with the local military officers who commanded the nearby garrison. In 1773, difficulties with Pedro Fages, the military commander, compelled Serra to travel to Mexico City to argue for the removal of Fages as the Governor of California Nueva. Viceroy Bucareli ruled in Serra's favor on 30 of the 32 charges brought against Fages, and removed him from office in 1774, after which time Serra could return to California.

Indians who were baptized were required to live at the mission and worked there as plowmen, shepherds, cattle herders, blacksmiths and carpenters. They were introduced to agricultural methods and tools that afforded them a better quality of life. Serra also successfully resisted the efforts of Governor Felipe de Neve to bring Enlightenment policies to missionary work because those policies would have subverted Serra's economic and religious goals. Serra wielded this kind of influence because his missions served economic and political purposes as well as religious ends. Economically, the missions produced all of the colony's cattle and grain on their own, and by the 1780s were even producing surpluses sufficient to trade with Mexico for luxury goods.

On August 28, 1784, Serra died at the age of 70 at Mission San Carlos, one of the missions he had founded. He was buried in the floor of the building there.

In 2015, during his first visit to the United States, Pope Francis made Junípero Serra a saint. The pontiff told the thousands who attended the Mass that Serra "sought to defend the dignity of the native community, to protect it from those who had mistreated and abused it. Mistreatment and wrongs which today still trouble us, especially because of the hurt which they cause in the lives of many people."

Junípero Serra is another one of those Catholics who changed the world we live in. He stressed the unity of the human race as one large family. He was granted the posthumous title *Apostle of California*.

59

Teresa of Calcutta: Who are the Poorest?

There is this well-known vase-and-faces drawing that provides a simple example of how we can switch between two views: our brain can switch from seeing the image as a vase to seeing it as two faces looking at each other. Obviously the drawing is made in such a way that it allows for two very different interpretations.

This image comes to mind when we want to talk about Mother Teresa. Some see her as a symbol of hope to many, as a saint who is even worshipped as a goddess by some Hindus. Others see her as a hindrance to rise above poverty, as someone who glorified illness and blessed poverty. It depends on which interpretation someone wants to see and foster. So who is the real Mother Teresa (1910-1997)?

Mother Teresa was born on August 26, 1910, in Skopje, the current capital of the Republic of Macedonia. The following day, she was baptized as Agnes Gonxha Bojaxhiu. Agnes left home in 1928 at age 18 to join the Sisters of Loreto in Ireland and to learn English with the view of becoming a missionary; English was the language of instruction of the Sisters of Loreto in India.

Teresa arrived in India in 1929, learnt Bengali, and became

59 Teresa of Calcutta: Who are the Poorest?

a teacher at the Loreto convent school in Calcutta (recently renamed Kolkata), the capital city of the Indian state of West Bengal. She chose to be named after Thérèse de Lisieux, the "Little Flower," but because a nun in the convent had already chosen that name, Agnes opted for its Spanish spelling (Teresa). Although Teresa enjoyed teaching at the school, she was increasingly disturbed by the poverty she witnessed in the surroundings of her school in Calcutta.

Teresa was still a young Loreto nun when she received "a call within a call" to found the Missionaries of Charity to serve "the poorest of the poor." So she began missionary work with the poor in 1948, replacing her traditional Loreto habit with a simple, white cotton sari with a blue border.

So difficult was the first year that she had to opt for begging. But it wasn't long before more young women joined her. Teresa adopted Indian citizenship, spent several months in Patna to receive basic medical training at Holy Family Hospital, and ventured into the slums. Teresa said, "By blood, I am Albanian. By citizenship, an Indian. By faith, I am a Catholic nun. As to my calling, I belong to the world. As to my heart, I belong entirely to the Heart of Jesus."

On October 7, 1950, Teresa received Vatican permission for her diocesan congregation which would become the *Missionaries of Charity*. In her own words, it would care for "the hungry, the naked, the homeless, the crippled, the blind, the lepers, all those people who feel unwanted, unloved, uncared for throughout society, people that have become a burden to the society and are shunned by everyone." The aim of the congregation was charity: homes for people dying of HIV/AIDS, leprosy and tuberculosis; soup kitchens; dispensaries and mobile clinics; children- and family-counselling programs; orphanages and schools. Members, who take vows of chastity, poverty and obedience, also profess a fourth vow: to give "wholehearted free service to the poorest of the poor."

In 1952, Teresa opened her first hospice with help from Calcutta officials. She converted an abandoned Hindu temple into the Kalighat Home for the Dying, free for the poor, and she renamed it Kalighat, the Home of the Pure Heart (Nirmal Hriday). Those brought to the home received medical attention and the opportunity to die with dignity in accordance with their faith: Muslims were read the Quran, Hindus received water from the Ganges, and Catholics received the last unction. "A beautiful death," Teresa said, "is for people who lived like animals to die like angels—loved and wanted."

The congregation began to attract recruits and donations, and by the 1960s it had opened hospices, orphanages and leper houses all over India. Teresa then expanded the congregation abroad, opening a house in Venezuela in 1965 with five sisters. Houses followed in Italy, Tanzania, and Austria in 1968, and during the 1970s the congregation opened houses and foundations in the United States and dozens of countries in Asia, Africa, and Europe. The congregation received a big boost after Malcolm Muggeridge's 1969 documentary *Something Beautiful for God*. The film was an important medium in drawing the Western world's attention to Mother Teresa.

Ten years later, Teresa received the Nobel Peace Prize "for work undertaken in the struggle to overcome poverty and distress, which also constitutes a threat to peace." She refused the conventional ceremonial banquet for laureates, asking that its $192,000 cost be given to the poor in India and saying that earthly rewards were important only if they helped her to help the world's needy. When Teresa received the prize, she was asked, "What can we do to promote world peace?" She answered, "Go home and love your family."

59 Teresa of Calcutta: Who are the Poorest?

For over 45 years, Mother Teresa served the poor, the sick, the dying, the orphaned and all those who had been rejected or abandoned. For Mother Teresa, the second greatest poverty in the world is the experience of being rejected and cast off by family and society. In her eyes, the greatest poverty is the spiritual emptiness that causes people to discard other human beings as useless objects. That's why Mother Teresa saw abortion as the worst example of poverty. "It is a poverty," she said, "to decide that a child must die so that you may live as you wish."

When she met Hillary Clinton in 1994, they obviously didn't agree on abortion (§47). When asked by Clinton why she thought the U.S. hasn't had a female president yet, Mother Teresa quipped back, "Because you probably aborted her." Yet, Mother Teresa assiduously sought Clinton's help in setting up a center in Washington, DC, where orphaned babies could be cared for, and later, in 1995, the Mother Teresa Home for Infant Children was founded.

At a National Prayer Breakfast hosted by the Clinton administration in 1994, Mother Teresa was invited to speak and she did not mince words about her feelings on abortion: "By abortion, the mother does not learn to love, but kills even her own child to solve her problems. And, by abortion, that father is told that he does not have to take any responsibility at all for the child he has brought into the world. The father is likely to put other women into the same trouble. So abortion just leads to more abortion. Any country that accepts abortion is not teaching its people to love, but to use any violence to get what they want. This is why the greatest destroyer of love and peace is abortion."

Gifted with keen intelligence, Mother Teresa led the expansion of her order to serve the poor, the sick, the dying and the orphaned. She did so for 45 years, until she resigned as head of the Missionaries of Charity. Today the order has over 4,500 Sisters and is active in 133 countries.

Shortly after her resignation, she died on September 5, 1997. Immediately after her death, Teresa lay in repose in St Thomas, Calcutta, for a week before her funeral. She received a state funeral from the Indian government in gratitude for her service to the poor of all religions in the country. Prime Minister of Pakistan Nawaz Sharif called her "a rare and unique individual who lived long for higher purposes. Her life-long devotion to the care of the poor, the sick and the disadvantaged was one of the highest examples of service to our humanity."

The world has not forgotten Mother Teresa since. She has been commemorated by museums and named the patroness of a number of churches. She has had buildings, roads and complexes named after her, including Albania's international airport. Mother Teresa Day ("Dita e Nënë Terezës"), on October 19, is a public holiday in Albania. In 2009, the Memorial House of Mother Teresa was opened in her hometown of Skopje, Macedonia.

To commemorate the 100th anniversary of her birth, the government of India issued a special ₹5 coin (the amount of money Teresa had when she arrived in India) on August 28, 2010. Indian Railways introduced the "Mother Express," a new train named after Mother Teresa, on August 26, 2010, to commemorate the centenary of her birth. The Tamil Nadu government organized centenary celebrations honoring Teresa on December 4, 2010, in Chennai, headed by chief minister M Karunanidhi. Beginning on September 5, 2013, the anniversary of her death has been designated the International Day of Charity by the UN General Assembly.

She also featured in several movies. Geraldine Chaplin

played Teresa in *Mother Teresa: In the Name of God's Poor*, which received a 1997 Art Film Festival award. She was also played by Olivia Hussey in a 2003 Italian television miniseries, *Mother Teresa of Calcutta*. Re-released in 2007, it received a CAMIE award. Teresa was played by Juliet Stevenson in the 2014 film *The Letters*, which was based on her letters to Vatican priest Celeste van Exem. They all show the stature of this great woman.

Mother Theresa is another one of those Catholics who changed the world we live in by serving the "poor," in the widest sense of the word. The impact of her and her sisters would soon be seen over the entire globe, from north to south, from east to west.

60

Thomas Aquinas: No Double Truth

Many people believe there is something like "double truth." Something can be true, but its opposite can be true too at the same time. They think that if evolution is true in science, then it may *not* be true when it comes to religion. Or they say that astronomy is true, but at the same time they still read their horoscopes because astrology is supposed to be as true as astronomy. Or they claim that Christianity, which believes in the Trinity, and Islam, which rejects the Trinity, can both be true. Or they believe that something can be fundamentally wrong according to sound morals, but at the same time fundamentally right in our actions. In politics, for instance, one can hold privately what one denies publicly—most of all, when it comes to abortion.

This has become known as the "double truth" approach. It may sound very attractive, and very convenient at times, but it has some serious flaws. The person who adamantly battled the "double truth" myth was Thomas Aquinas (1225-1274).

Aquinas was born at Roccasecca, a hilltop castle from which the great Benedictine abbey of Montecassino (§9) is almost visible, midway between Rome and Naples. At the age of five, he entered at Montecassino where his studies began. When the monastery became a battle site, Thomas was transferred by his family to the University of Naples. It was there that he came into contact with the philosopher Aristotle and with the Order of Preachers or Dominicans, a recently founded mendicant order. He became a Dominican over the protests of his family and eventually went north to study, perhaps first briefly at Paris, then at Cologne with Albert the Great (§1). It was Albert's interest in Aristotle that would strengthen Thomas's own fascination with Aristotle.

After returning to Paris, he completed his studies, and for three years, occupied one of the Dominican chairs in the Faculty of Theology. The next ten years were spent in various places in Italy, at various Dominican houses, and eventually in Rome. From there he was called back to Paris. After this second three-year period, he was assigned to Naples. In 1274, on his way to the Council of Lyon, he fell ill and died on March 7 in the Cistercian abbey at Fossanova, some 20 kilometers from his home town Roccasecca.

He was described by G. K. Chesterton (§17) as "a huge heavy bull of a man, fat and slow and quiet, very mild and magnanimous but not very sociable." His fellow Dominican friars referred to him as "the dumb ox," to which his teacher Albert the Great responded that "the dumb ox will bellow so loud that his bellowing will fill the world." Those words were prophetic. Although a man of profound humility and prayerful contemplation, Aquinas was also a pioneering genius whose writings constitute the apotheosis of medieval thought and the embryonic beginnings of a world-wide innovation.

The philosophy of Thomas Aquinas has so many facets and has survived more than seven centuries. Its impact has gone up and down, but always came out stronger than ever. Here we will only focus on one aspect of his philosophy. At the time of

Thomas Aquinas, Islamic philosophers had introduced the idea that there can be "double truth." This meant that religious knowledge and philosophical knowledge may arrive at different, contradictory truths, but without detriment to each other. By placing the "truths" of philosophy and science in one category and the "truths" of faith and religion in another, one could hold mutually exclusive positions as long as one believes that the opposing views are in separate departments of the mind—one for Sundays and one for weekdays, so to speak. Truth allegedly depends on how you look at it.

Here is an example from Islam: Allah could will one thing today and its opposite tomorrow. Allah's latest affirmation is true for now, but it can change the following day, of course. According to this view, since truth is not grounded in our "reasoning," but in Allah's "willing," the only way we could know that the sun will arise in the morning is if Allah wills it and we believe it. This means that we cannot really rely on "nature" for anything. This may sound strange to us, but many politicians, too, use the double truth position when it comes to something like abortion. If abortion is wrong in one's personal life, it can still be right in one's political life.

Aquinas considered the idea of "double truth" unsustainable. He saw with utter clarity that all truth comes from God, and therefore there can never be, ultimately, any conflict between one truth and another truth—between what we know though science and what we know through Scripture, or between philosophical truths and theological truths, or between yesterday's truths and todays' truths. He claimed that faith and science, or theology and philosophy, play, in Aquinas' own words, "complementary roles in the quest for truth. Grace does not destroy nature but fulfills it."

We have the Catholic Church, and Thomas Aquinas in

particular, to thank for constantly reminding us that all truth is God's truth. and is therefore universal, global, and unchanging. God has revealed himself both in the Scriptures and in the natural world. Therefore, if we find a seeming contradiction between the two, then we have not understood correctly either the Scriptures or the natural world, or both.

Perhaps a few examples may demonstrate how important the rejection of "double truth" is. It cannot be, for instance, that the earth is flat according to faith and religion, but at the same time spherical according to reason and science, for that would create a contradiction. In a similar way, if science tells us that the earth circles the sun, it cannot be true also that the sun circles the earth. In all such cases we are dealing with contradictions which cannot both be true at the same time given the fact that there is no "double truth." When we detect a "double truth," either one or both must have been claimed in error and must be reevaluated.

One word of caution, though. Sometimes we might think we have a double-truth issue, when in fact we do not. For instance, creation as understood by faith versus the Big Bang theory as understood by science do not contradict each other (§43). The Big Bang is about the *beginning* of the universe—about how physical interactions came about—whereas faith in creation is about the *origin* of the universe—about how the Universe is ultimately dependent on God.

Here is another example. Creation, as understood by faith, versus evolution, as understood by science, do not contradict each other. Creation is about how all natural causes are related to God, whereas evolution deals with how natural causes are related to each other through reproduction and natural selection. The same can be said about randomness in science and Providence in faith. Randomness is about how events can be related to each other, whereas Providence is about how events are related to God. So we do not need to make a choice between two truths in these cases because there is no problem of "double truth" here.

How important the rejection of "double truth" is can be seen when we weigh it against contrary views. Some believers—such as the Protestant Reformer Martin Luther in his more excitable moments—have held that faith at all times trumps reason. Others have held—especially so nowadays—that science must always trump faith if religion is to survive in the modern world. Contrary to these views, Thomas Aquinas and the Catholic Church claim that the truths of faith must agree with the truths of science because God is author of both, and so any apparent conflict between them shows that we have failed to understand one or the other or both. If something is true in philosophy or science, it must also be true in the Christian faith. Truth is truth, as all truth is God's truth—although we may not fully grasp the full truth yet.

The idea of "double truth" may seem obsolete, but nowadays it has come back in a new disguise of "multiple truths." It's called relativism. A relativist claims that there is no absolute truth—there are only opinions about what is true, depending on one's point of view. What's wrong with that? Well, if the world is not flat, someone's opinion will not make it flat. Opinions don't trump truths. Besides, the statement "all truth is relative" leads to a contradiction. Denying that there is objective truth means you are insisting in your denial that what you say is objectively true, which cannot be true by its own verdict. To say that "all truth is relative" amounts to saying that we have no way of knowing what is true. But then we have no way either of knowing that the claim of "all truth is relative" is true.

So the idea of "multiple truths" is as flawed as the idea of "double truth." Let's state it again, truth is truth, even if you do not accept it; and untruth is untruth, even if you claim it. Truth is not something we create or invent, but something that we try to discover and "capture." Truth is truth—for everyone, anywhere, at any time. Aquinas had told us that already some eight centuries ago.

Thomas Aquinas is another one of those Catholics who changed the world we live in. He showed us that "truth is truth" and that all truth comes from God and that we had better adjust to the truth.

Conclusion

It seems to me that the best way to bring this book to a close is using a quote from Tom Peterson (*MyGodsBlog.com*) about Catholics and the Catholic Church:

> *Our family is made up of every race. We are young and old, men and women, sinners and saints. Our family has spanned the centuries and the globe. With God's grace, we started hospitals to care for the sick. We establish orphanages and help the poor. We are the largest charitable organization on the planet, bringing relief and comfort to those in need. We educate more children than any other scholarly or religious institution. We developed the scientific method and laws of evidence. We founded the college system. We defend the dignity of all human life and uphold marriage and family. Cities were named after our revered saints, who navigated a sacred path before us. Guided by the Holy Spirit, we compiled the Bible. We are transformed by sacred Scripture and sacred Tradition, which have consistently guided us for two thousand years. We are the Catholic Church, with over one billion in our family sharing in the sacraments and fullness of Christian faith.*

Index

A

abortion 28, 65, 66, 204-6, 220, 233-4, 261, 264, 266
addictions 89, 91
Albert the Great 1, 3, 265
Alcoholics Anonymous ... 90
Alcuin of York 4-6
ambulance 50-52
Anselm 13-15, 174
apologetics 172, 192-5
Aquinas, Thomas ....
    31, 77, 174, 183, 196, 199, 201, 209, 219, 264-9
Arianism 16-21, 75, 123
Aristotle . 2, 77, 79, 180, 265
Athanasius of Alexandria 16-21
atheism 88, 168-9, 193, 196
Augustine 26, 86, 124, 173-4, 184, 220

B

Bede the Venerable . 25, 145
Bellarmine, Robert 28-32
Belloc, Hilaire 20, 248
Benedict of Nursia. 33-4, 37
Benedict XVI ....
    .... 65, 126, 152, 169, 216

Bennett, Rod 226
Big Bang 180-5, 267
blood transfusions 177-8
Bosco, John 38-40
Brandsma, Titus 41-6

C

Cafasso, Joseph 47-9
Camillus de Lellis 50-2
Canisius, Peter 53-8, 158
capitalism ....
    87, 169, 186-90, 210, 243
Carrel, Alexis 59-64
catechism 53-8, 73, 170
Catherine of Siena 65-7
Charlemagne 5, 27, 127
Check, Christopher 67
Chesterton, G.K. 60, 68-70, 190, 194, 196-7, 208-9, 216, 248, 265
church and state ....
    .... 124, 126, 130
Claver, Peter 71-3
colonization 113-5
common sense 68-70
Communism 1
    ...... 60, 165-70, 188, 190
concordats 237-8

Constantine 19, 74-6
contraception .220-1, 233-5
Copernicus, Nicolaus .. 77-9
Cornwell, John 239
Council in Jerusalem ... 230
Cyril and Methodius.. 81-82

D

Damien de Veuster 83-5
Day, Dorothy 86, 88
distributism 87
Douay-Rheims Bible . 143-4
double truth 264-9
Dowling, Edward 89-91
Drexel, Katharine 92-4
Duhem, Pierre 95-100
Dulles, Avery 32

E

Easter 136
Edict of Milan 76
Einstein, Albert ....
.... 95, 180-2, 210
entitlements 28, 203
EWTN 11,

F

fair wage 190, 244,
faith and reason ....
.... 4, 171, 173-5
feminism 65-7
Francis of Assisi 101-6

Francis Xavier 84, 107-11
freedom of expression . 41-3
freedom of religion .. 216-20

G

Galileo Galilei 77-9, 81
genetics 213-5
globalization 246
González, Roque 113
Grant, Edward 98
Greene, Graham 116-20
Gregorian calendar ....
.... 26, 132-7, 160
Gregory the Great ....
.... 107, 121-5, 127, 134
Gregory VII 126-131
Gregory XIII 29, 132-7
Gutenberg Bible 140
Gutenberg, Johannes ..138-
140, 143, 151, 210

H

heliocentrism 77-9
Hieronymus 141
Hildegard of Bingen 147-52
history 25
Hitler 42, 237-42
Hochhuth, Rolf 241-2
Holocaust 239-40
hospice 260
hospital ... 33-7, 50-2, 61, 85

272

Index

I

Ignatius of Antioch.....153-5
Ignatius of Loyola...............
.... 54, 108, 156-161
Incarnation.................. 17-8
Industrial Revolution...187, 191
infection 83, 249-53
Internet ....
..7, 101, 164, 207-8, 210
Investiture Controversy 127
Isidore of Seville............162
Islam....16-21, 97-99, 264-6

J

Jerome.................. 81, 141-6
Jesuits...............................
56, 59, 72, 107-11, 114-5, 156-60
John of Damascus.......... 20
John Paul II.......................
4, 11, 57, 66, 82, 104-105, 164-170, 175, 191
journalism ..7-8, 42, 45, 116
Judaism 16-7, 225, 228
Julian calendar........ 132-37
Justin the Martyr 171-6

K

King James Bible...........146
Kreeft, Peter 1, 196, 236
Kuhn, Thomas................ 98

L

Landsteiner, Karl....... 177-9
Lemaître, Georges 180
Leo XIII ....
27, 86-7, 93, 186-91, 244, 248
leprosy 83-85, 222, 259
Lewis, C.S......18, 193, 196-7
Lincoln, Abraham...... 15, 71
living wage 244-5
Lourdes....................... 60-3
Luther, Martin...................
54-5, 78, 140, 145, 175, 268

M

Maritain, Jacques ....
.... 29, 198-203
Marxism................ 168, 186
mass communication ...7-8, 56
materialism............. 69, 189
Mauriac, François..............
.... 116-7, 119
McCorvey, Norma 204-6
McLuhan, Marshall . 207-11
Mendel, Gregor.......... 213-5
micro-organisms 222-4
minimum wage..........243-5
miracles 59-64, 195, 225
monotheism................16, 21
Monte Cassino 34-5

More, Thomas 218-20
Mother Angelica 8, 10-2
Mother Teresa 258-63

N
natural law.... 189, 201, 203
nature 92-106
Nazism 42, 186, 237, 247
Newman, John Henry .. 119, 221
Nicene Creed 18, 20, 154
Nietzsche, Friedrich 202

O
O'Flaherty, Hugh 240
Oppenheimer, J. Robert 98
out of nothing 17, 182-3

P
Pacepa, Ion 242
papal authority ....
.... 121, 124, 130, 219-20
Pasteur, Louis ....
.... 96, 222-4, 254
Paul of Tarsus 225, 230
Paul VI. 117, 167, 231-2, 236
Pearce, Joseph 118
Pius XI 86, 225, 238-9,
Pius XII ... 232, 237, 239-42
polymath 2, 148, 151, 160
printing press ....
.... 53-5, 138-9, 143

prisons 38, 47-9
Protestantism ..56, 158, 210
Ptolemy 77

R
Red Cross 50-2
Reductions 113-5
Reformation ....
.... 53-6, 145, 155, 219
relativism 68, 268
religious liberty 216, 220
Roe v. Wade 205
Roman Catholic ....
... 69, 155, 178, 209, 250
Ryan, John Augustan 243-5

S
Sartre, Jean-Paul 202
schools ....
4-5, 23-4, 80, 85, 94, 96-7, 107, 111, 139, 143, 157, 159, 162-4, 218, 236, 238, 259
Schumacher, E.F. 246-8
science ....
1-3, 22, 59, 62, 70, 92, 95-101, 151-2, 160, 164, 173, 179, 183-4, 199, 210, 214-5, 224, 264, 266-8
Semmelweis, Ignaz . 249-54
Septuagint 142
Serra, Junípero 255-7

Sexual Revolution 186, 204, 231-5
skepticism 68, 70
slave trade 13-5, 71-3
slavery 13-5
social justice 86, 88, 189
social media............... 207-9
social teaching 31-2, 87-8, 186, 191, 245
socialism 87, 170, 186-91
Solzhenitsyn, Aleksandr..... 168
Stark, Rodney 97
subsidiarity........ 190-1, 248
Suetonius...................... 228
supremacy 127, 219

T

Thomas Aquinas .... See Aquinas, Thomas
Trinitarianism 19
twelve steps 89-91

U

urbanization 38, 40, 101, 190

V

vernacular.......................... ....53, 55, 80-2, 142, 145
Vulgate 81, 140-5

W

welfare state.................. 243
Whitehead, Alfred North 98

X

Xavier University............ 94

275

Praise for the Book

"Taken from various times and places, we have here specifically Catholics who, in their works and lives, have improved the world in one way or another. Many good things need to be invented, begun, organized, or planned. We have here a welcome reflection on who such people are and what they did because of their Catholic outlook on the world."
— James V. Schall, S.J., Professor Emeritus, Georgetown University († 2019).

"These 60 Catholics truly did change the world for the better, and any Catholic can at the least change his or her world for the better. May these 60 give you inspiration in your own life–I know they have in mine!"
— Dr. Sebastian Mahfood, OP, co-author with Bishop Richard Henning of *Missionary Priests in the Homeland*

About the Author

Gerard M. Verschuuren is a human biologist, specialized in human genetics. He also earned a doctorate in the philosophy of science. He studied and worked at universities in Europe and the United States. Currently semi-retired, he spends most of his time as a writer, speaker, and consultant on the interface of science and religion, faith and reason.

Some of his most recent books are:

- *God and Evolution?—Science Meets Faith.* (Boston, MA: Pauline Books, 2012).
- *The Destiny of the Universe—In Pursuit of the Great Unknown.* (St. Paul, MN: Paragon House, 2014).
- *Life's Journey—A Guide from Conception to Growing Up, Growing Old, and Natural Death.* (Kettering, OH: Angelico Press, 2016).
- *Aquinas and Modern Science—A New Synthesis of Faith and Reason.* (Kettering, OH: Angelico Press, 2016).
- *Faith and Reason—The Cradle of Truth.* (St. Louis, MO: En Route Books and Media, 2017).
- *The Myth of an Anti-Science Church—Galileo,*

- *Darwin, Teilhard, Hawking, Dawkins.* (Kettering, OH: Angelico Press, 2018).
- *The First Christians—Keeping the Faith in Times of Trouble.* (St. Louis, MO: En Route Books and Media, 2018).
- *The Eclipse of God—Is Religion on the Way out?* (St. Louis, MO: En Route Books and Media, 2018).
- *Forty Anti-Catholic Lies.* (Manchester, NH: Sophia Institute Press, 2018).
- *In the Beginning—A Catholic Scientist Explains How God Made Earth Our Home.* (Manchester, NH: Sophia Institute Press, 2019).
- *Broken Hearts in a Broken World.* (St. Louis, MO: En Route Books and Media, 2019).
- *The Destructive Doctrines of Our Age.* (St. Louis, MO: En Route Books and Media, 2019).
- *At the Dawn of Humanity—The First Humans.* (Kettering, OH: Angelico Press, 2020).

For more info:
http://en.wikipedia.org/wiki/Gerard_Verschuuren

Dr. Verschuuren may be contacted at
www.where-do-we-come-from.com

www.ingramcontent.com/pod-product-compliance
Lightning Source LLC
Chambersburg PA
CBHW032150080426
42735CB00008B/650